KODAK

Pocket Guide to Point-and-Shoot Photography

KODAK Pocket Guide to Point-and-Shoot Photography

ISBN 0-87985-811-7

Design: Andrea Zocchi Design
Printed in the United States of America

Kodak
LICENSED PRODUCT

Library of Congress Control Number 00-133491

KODAK Books are published under license
from Eastman Kodak Company by
Silver Pixel Press®
A Tiffen® Company
21 Jet View Drive
Rochester, NY 14624 USA
Fax: (716) 328-5078
www.silverpixelpress.com

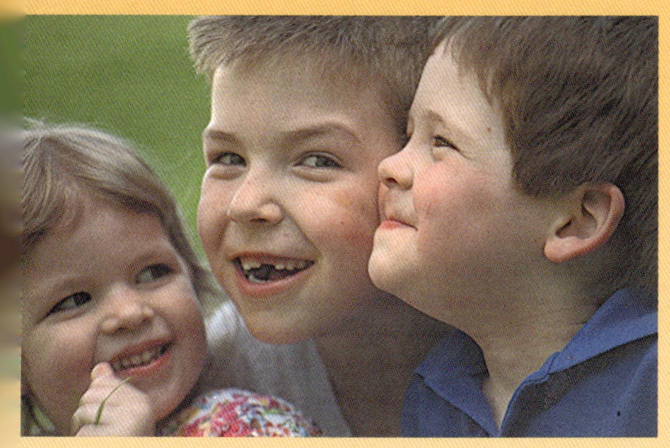

Contents

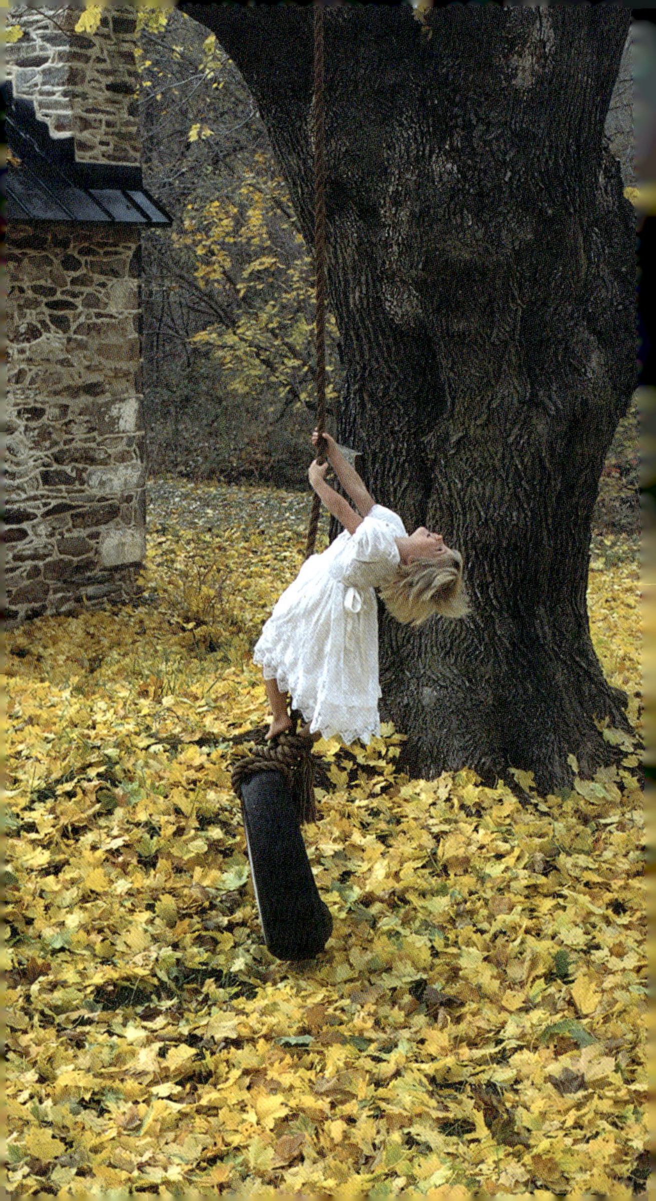

Introduction

When I first became interested in photography, I thought that to take good photographs I had to buy a lot of expensive equipment and master complicated photographic techniques. I've since realized this isn't true. Outstanding images can be made with even the most basic point-and-shoot camera and this book is full of examples

Learning how to improve your photography is easier than you might guess. First you need to learn about a few of your camera's functions. That will improve the technical aspects of your photography. It's amazing how well today's small point-and-shoot cameras can perform when used properly.

The second part of great point-and-shoot photography is really the artistry of photography. There are a few tricks and techniques you can use to vastly improve everyday pictures. And an understanding of what makes an image good will help you integrate these aspects into your own photographs.

Perhaps the most important thing is to make photography part of your lifestyle. You won't take good pictures if your camera stays in a drawer somewhere. Improving your pictures takes practice, and daily life can be the best subject. Years from now you'll be glad you have them.

Short of Time?
Five Quick Tips to Improve Your Photos

Are you excited to get out and start taking pictures? Maybe there is an important event you want to photograph, but you won't have time to read this whole book first. Take a little time to learn these five quick tips. They can teach you a few tricks for taking better photographs.

1. Focus Lock Function

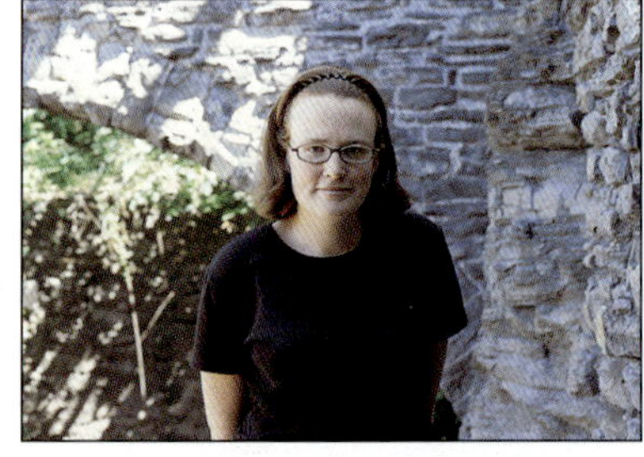

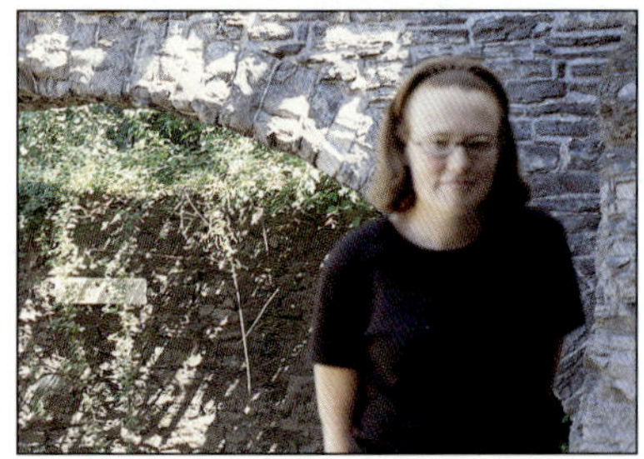

Most point-and-shoot cameras have a heavily centered autofocusing system. What is in the center of your viewfinder when you take the picture, is what will be in the sharpest focus. Sometimes it won't make a difference, but if your subject isn't centered, it can be a disaster.

Use your camera's FOCUS-LOCK function to avoid this problem.

2. When In Doubt, Use Fill Flash

Flash is not just for indoor and night photography. Fill-flash can be very effective in sunny conditions to soften harsh shadows on your subject's face and add snap to pictures taken on overcast days. When in doubt, use the fill-flash function on your camera. If your camera doesn't have fill-flash, take one photo with auto flash and one without.

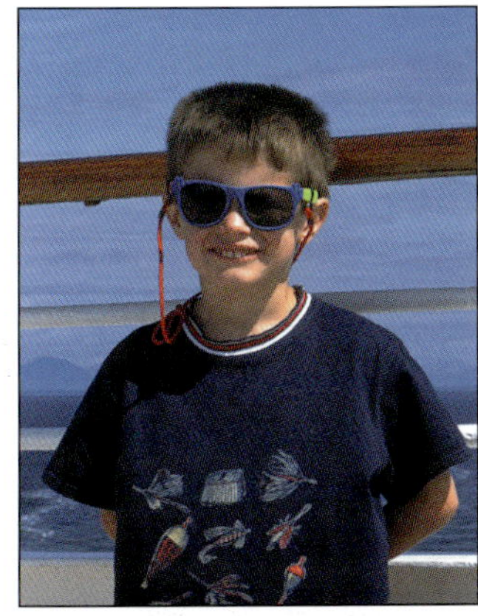

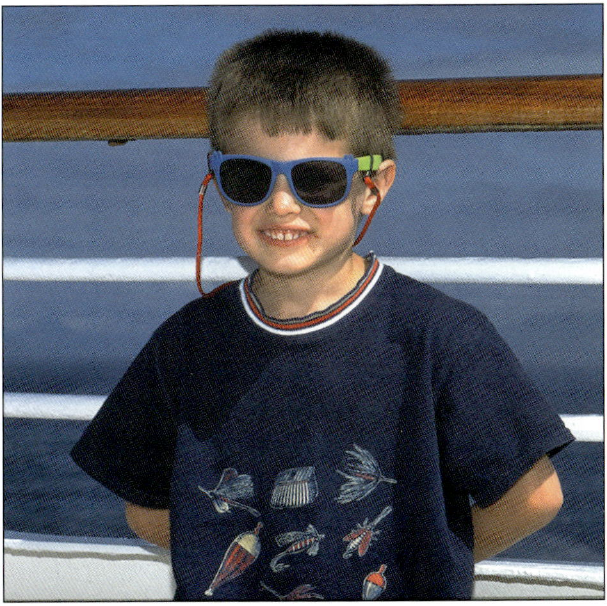

3. The Rule of Thirds

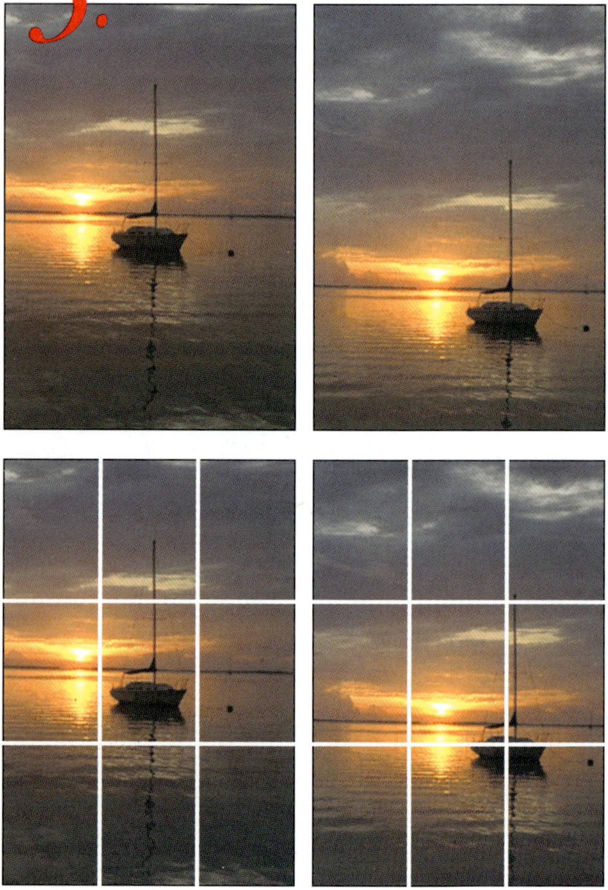

Don't center your subject or position the horizon line through the middle of the photo. For better compositions, imagine the scene divided into thirds and place key elements along the dividing lines or at the junction points.

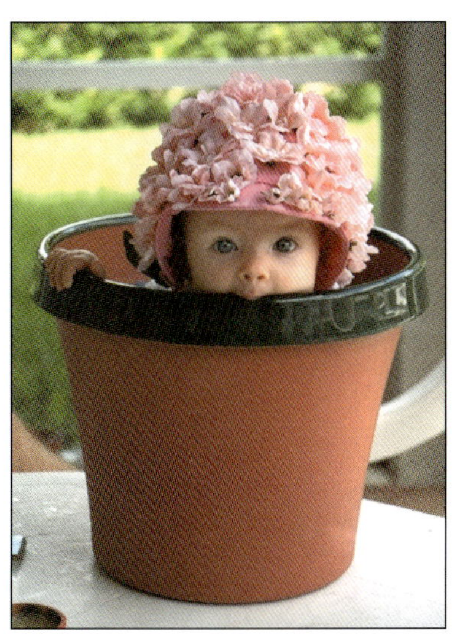

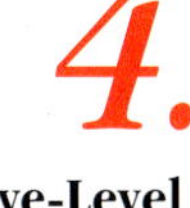

Eye-Level

A big improvement can be made in most portraiture if you shoot at your subject's eye level. This means with kids or seated adults, you need to crouch down; with taller folks you should stand on your toes; and with infants you might need to lay on your belly.

5. Use Quality Photofinishing

Bad looking photos might not be your fault if your composition is strong. Quality photofinishing can turn a so-so picture into a stunning image, by avoiding common problems like ugly color casts, lack of contrast (or too much contrast), and overly dark or light prints. You might not even realize the potential lost in bad printing unless you compared it to a properly printed picture.

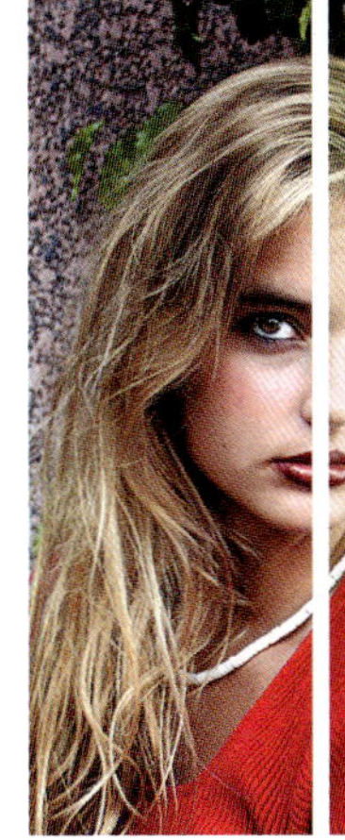

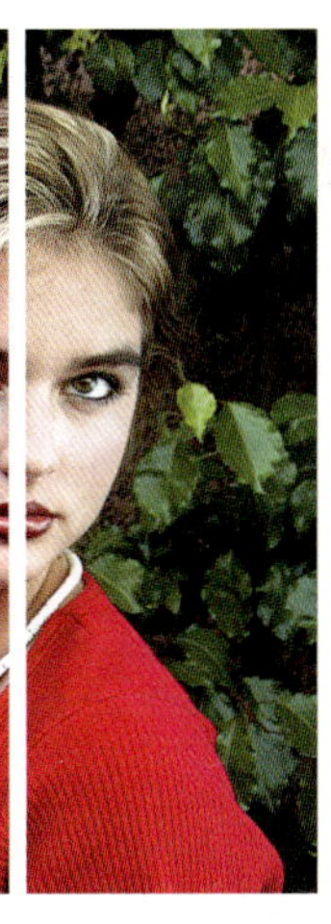

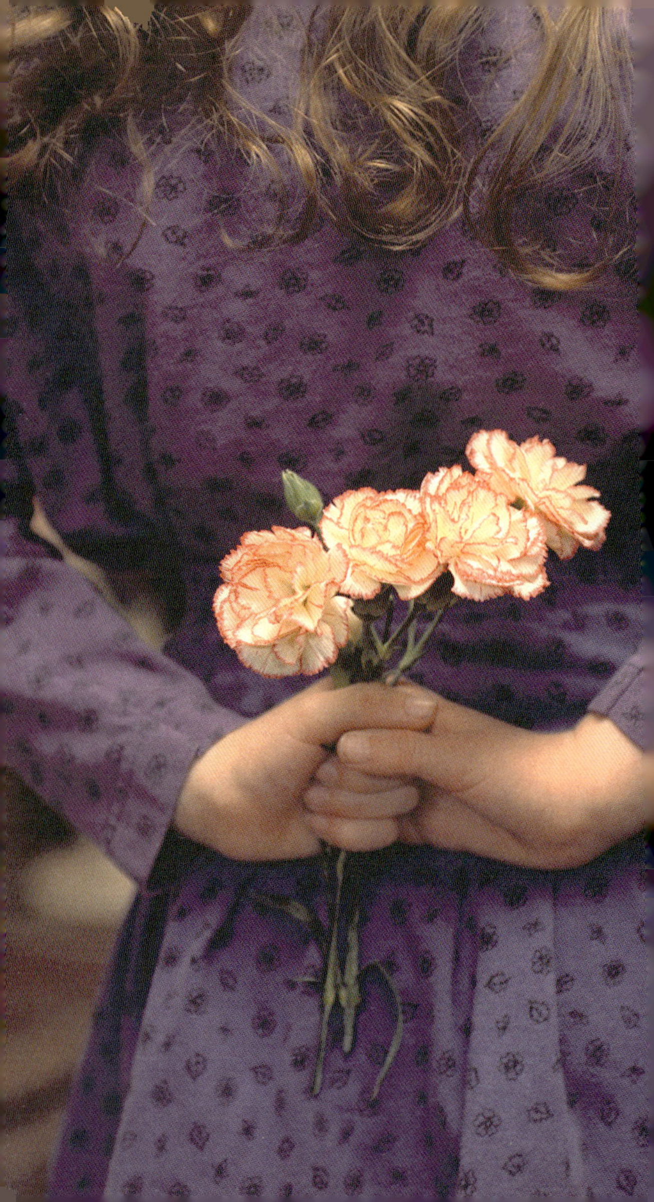

What Kind of Camera Should I Buy?

Whether you would like to upgrade your current camera or are a first-time buyer, there are several things you need to consider including camera type, size, price, ease of use, and features.

Point-and-Shoot Cameras

The most popular cameras are the compact point-and-shoot variety. Technically, they are called lens-shutter cameras. Aside from being small and having "auto everything" simplicity, they are differentiated by the fact that when you look through the viewfinder, you are not actually looking through the camera's lens. This explains why you can have your finger over the lens and never see it in the viewfinder; or accidentally cut off a person's head in the final picture, though you know you saw it in the viewfinder.

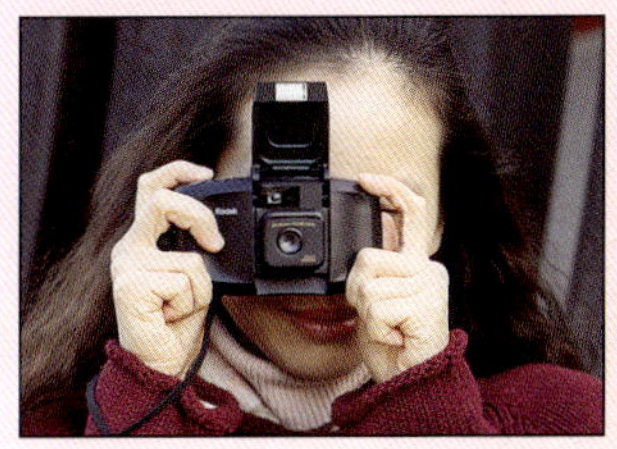

Point-and-shoot cameras are generally small and easy to use.

Point-and-shoot cameras are extremely popular because they come in a very small package and are easy to use. Some of the latest Advanced Photo System point-and-shoot cameras are the width and height of a credit card, and less than an inch thick.

Plus, the better point-and-shoot cameras can deliver some exceptional results. Most professional photographers can boast at least a few saleable images that they took with their "snapshot" cameras. Manufacturers are continually adding new features, and improving the exposure, focusing, flash and other capabilities of these easy-to-use cameras.

However, even the most sophisticated point-and-shoot cameras lack some of the capabilities and conveniences of their much larger SLR (single-lens reflex) counterparts.

SLR Cameras

Single-lens-reflex (SLR) cameras are generally considered "professional" cameras, but there are many that are in the same price range as high-end point-and-shoot cameras. SLR cameras offer a lot of sophisticated user-selectable controls that are beyond the scope of this book, but the big difference between an SLR and a point-and-shoot camera is the ability to change from one lens to another whenever you want. They also have a viewfinder that sees through-the-lens (TTL) for WYSIWYG (What-You-See-Is-What-You-Get) accuracy. When used in "auto" or program mode, however, these cameras work very much like high-end point-and-shoot cameras.

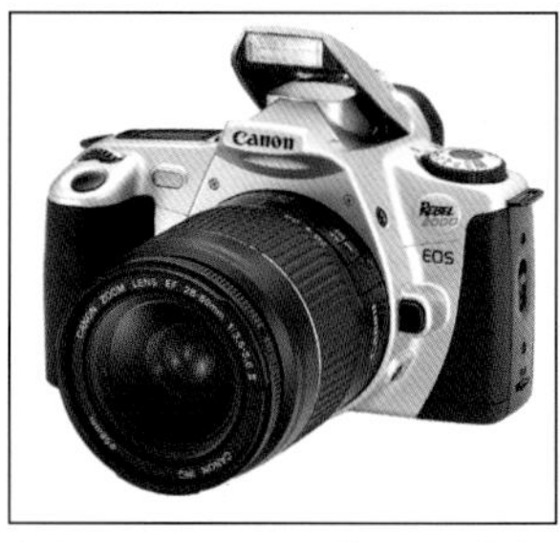

SLR cameras can be used in point-and-shoot "auto" mode, however, they are far larger and heavier than their compact cousins.

Advanced Photo System Film Cameras

The Advanced Photo System is a relatively new camera/film system that offers many consumer benefits. The biggest difference is that APS films have a special magnetic layer not found on ordinary 35mm film that allows Information Exchange (IX) with the camera and the photofinishing lab equipment. This data helps to improve print quality and enables some of the advanced functions.

If you've looked at these cameras, you are probably amazed by their small size, made possible by the unique shape of the film cassette. This cassette is also the film storage vessel after processing, meaning you never have to handle negatives again.

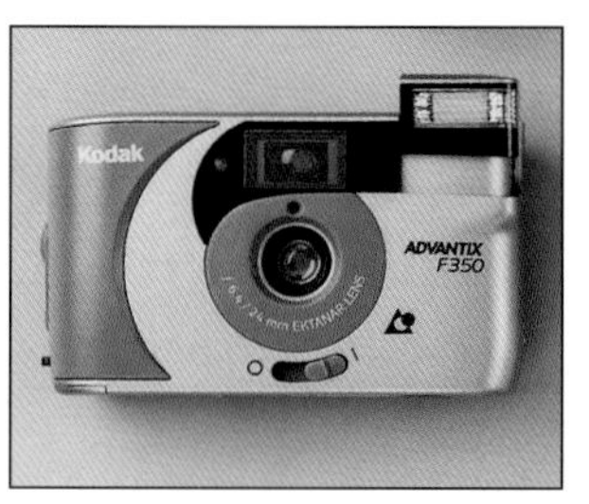

Advanced Photo System cameras tend to be incredibly compact and lightweight.

Indexing printing is a nice perk, because it makes reprinting your favorite pictures a breeze. The index print shows a miniature version of each frame, along with the frame number and cassette ID (see page 29). Just pick the picture you like from the image on the index print, match the ID number, drop the cassette off at the lab, and you can get reprints without ever having to touch, look at, or sort the negatives!

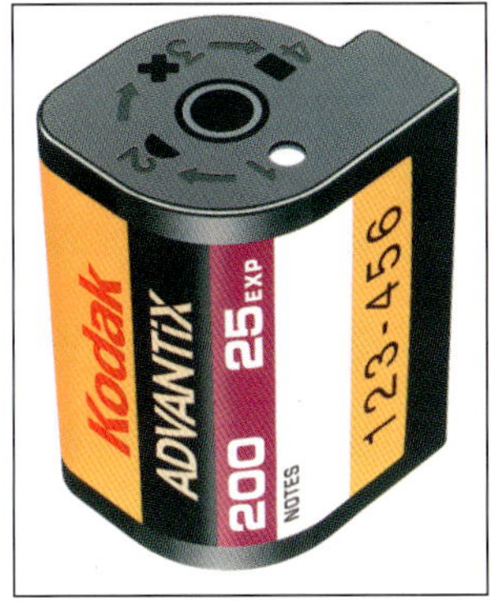

The Advanced Photo System film canister has a unique design and is considerably smaller than a 35mm film cassette, which explains why APS cameras can be so tiny.

Most APS cameras are the point-and-shoot type, although a few manufacturers offer SLR versions. APS cameras all feature drop-in film loading, and most give you an exposure countdown, so you always know how many shots you have left. Some allow you to set captions that are automatically printed by the lab on the back of your photographs.

Perhaps the most enjoyable feature of most Advanced Photo System cameras is the choice of three print formats. This gives you the creative advantage of being able to design your photographs as traditional ratio (4x6-inch Classic format) prints, as slightly wider ratio (H-format) prints, or in a much wider double size (Panoramic) prints. For a full discussion of print formats, see the APS Print Formats section on page 14.

35mm Film Cameras

35mm film cameras have been the most popular film type for decades, and they are therefore very familiar. Numerous color print films and a wide variety of consumer slide films, specialty films, and professional films are available. (See the section on films on pages 27–28 for more details.) Most 35mm film cameras come in both point-and-shoot and SLR models.

APS Print Formats

APS cameras usually offer a choice of three print formats, while some "panoramic" 35mm cameras offer two. Changing the print format is one of the quickest ways to alter the look of your photos.

Standard 4x6 C-Format

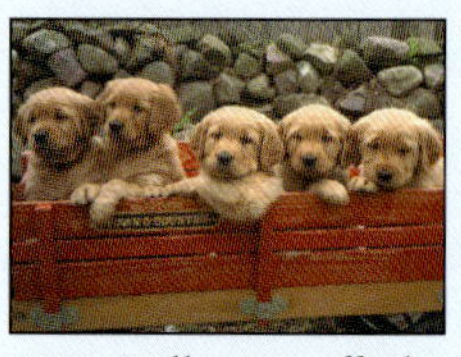

The most familiar format is Classic or C-format, since it corresponds proportionately to the 3-1/2x5-inch or the 4x6-inch prints we are accustomed to seeing. It is important to note, however, that the Classic-format print actually crops off a little bit of the image from the sides.

Wider 4x7 H-Format

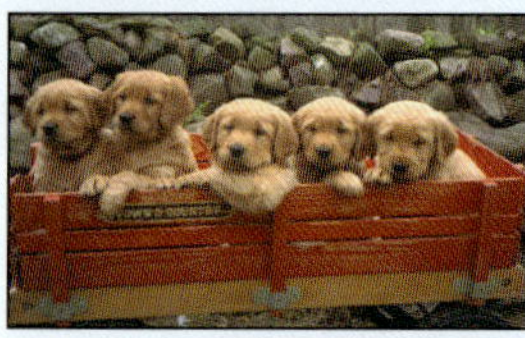

H-format is an exclusive APS format. The print has the same ratio as the film negative and the image is not cropped. On the index print, the whole unmarked image is the H-format.

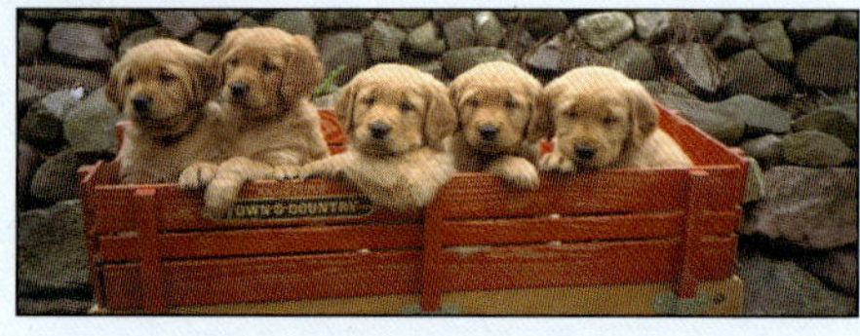

The Extra-Wide Panoramic P-Format

At almost double the width of the 4x6-inch Classic format, the Panoramic format gives you huge prints that add impact to your family album or look great in a frame. It is especially effective for group pictures, sweeping scenics that include cloudless sky, and vertical shots of tall subjects like trees and people.

Digital Cameras

Digital cameras also run the gamut from point-and-shoot varieties, to high-end SLRs and other professional versions. There are even digital imaging attachments for your Palm Pilot!

All digital cameras share the advantage of eliminating the expense of film and processing, although there are expenses in the form of batteries, storage media, ink-jet printing papers and inks. Instead of taking film to the lab, digital images can be transferred to your computer, output on a printer, and e-mailed to friends and family.

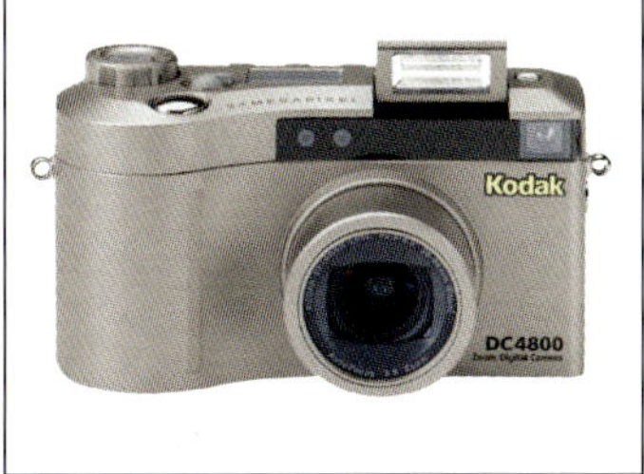

Digital cameras give instant gratification, and allow you to share pictures over the Internet within minutes.

Digital cameras come in low-resolution models (under one million pixels), which are good for e-mail and internet fun, as well as small prints. Megapixel cameras offer higher resolution for larger, better printouts. A 3-megapixel digital camera will meet the needs of most consumers, including making photographic-quality prints.

Most digital cameras have a big advantage over film cameras in that they give instant gratification—you know if you got the shot or not, because you can view it on the built-in monitor. This means you can share the results instantly with your subject. And if both photographer and subject aren't happy with the outcome, you can erase the picture instantly and try again. And if the results are good, even the most reticent model can become extremely enthusiastic.

Don't overlook the e-mail advantage either. Today's digital cameras offer quick and easy downloading to a computer. This means you can e-mail pictures to friends and family all over the world, just seconds after you take them. See page 89 for more information on digital photography, or check out the *KODAK Pocket Guide to Digital Photography*.

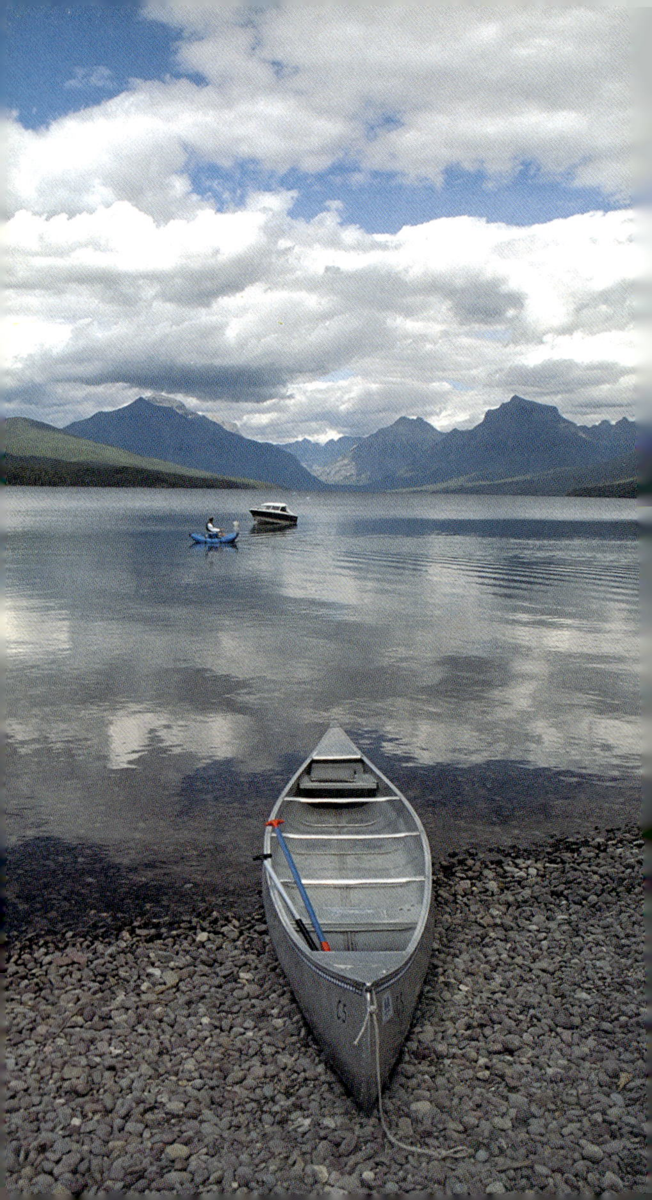

Selecting a Camera

Once you know the basic type of camera you want (35mm, Advanced Photo System, or Digital), there are other factors to consider. The most obvious is cost—how much (or little) do you have to spend to get a camera that fits your needs. The size and "feel" are important. Is the camera so small that you can't hold it without covering important parts with your hands? Or is it so big that you never want to carry it?

Specifications and features are also important. The following sections describe what all the "bells and whistles" really do—from lenses, to flash, to print format choices.

Lens Selection

Wide, Normal, or Telephoto: The focal length of your lens indicates the magnification and field of view that your camera sees. Wide-angle lenses see a wide expanse, but distant objects seem especially small and far away. "Normal" lenses show the world pretty much as our eyes see it, without the peripheral vision. Telephoto or "long" lenses magnify the subject, and make them seem closer in the picture.

Single Focal Length Cameras

The most economical point-and-shoot cameras have only one lens setting, and it's usually normal or slightly wide-angle. This is good for scenic photography, photographing groups of people, and general indoor photography.

Dual Focal Length Cameras

Two lens settings on these cameras give you more versatility, because you can switch between views (usually normal and wide-angle, or normal and telephoto).

Zoom Lenses

The ability to zoom from wide angle to telephoto is a big advantage, because you get a lot more control over image composition with dozens of focal lengths to chose from. See the sidebar on page 20 for examples.

Interchangeable Lenses

Most cameras with interchangeable lenses are larger SLR cameras that are beyond the scope of this book. However, because they can be used in "point-and-shoot" auto modes, they are included here. Being able to change lenses gives you a great opportunity to control your composition, because you can pick anything from super-wide "fisheye" lenses, to telephotos that can give you a head shot of a distant bird, or even an attachment for a microscope.

Other Lens Factors

Many people buy a camera without giving much thought to the lens in terms of quality and speed. The quality factor is obvious—a cheap camera with a plastic lens cannot possibly produce images with the same color, contrast, and sharpness of a quality glass lens.

Speed (or how much light the lens can gather) is an often overlooked specification on a camera. However, it can have a major effect on overall picture quality. A cheaper, "slow" lens will require you to use faster than normal film speeds, which results in an overall drop in quality. (See the Films section on pages 27–28.) It also means you'll need to use slower shutter speeds, and risk blurred images or have to use flash when you normally wouldn't need it.

Exposure Modes

A few high-end cameras have special Exposure Modes. These functions help you get better exposures in specialized situations, such as Portraiture (when an out-of-focus, soft background is preferable), Landscape (for pictures that are crystal sharp from foreground to background), and Close-Up Mode (for a closer look at flowers and other small subjects). For example, in Landscape Mode, the camera settings keep everything from foreground to background in sharp focus. But in portrait mode, it is just the opposite; the camera settings

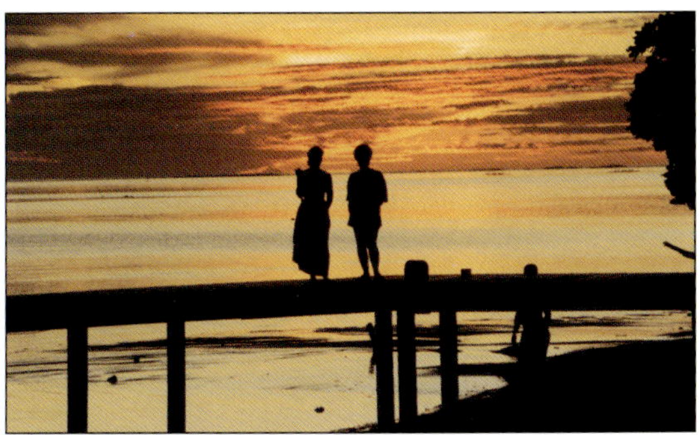
Wide-angle lens setting

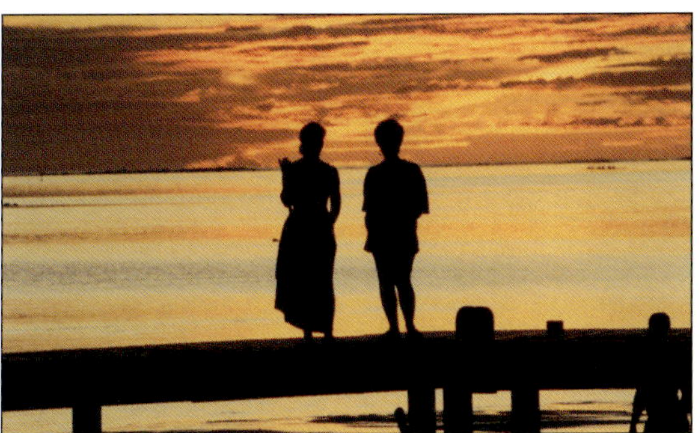
Normal lens setting

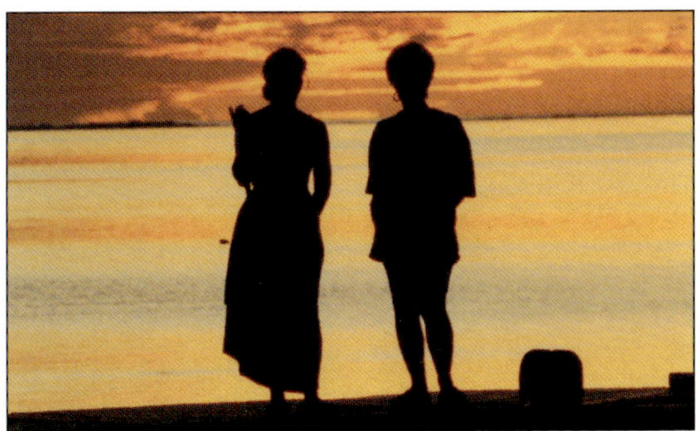
Telephoto lens setting

Creative Composition with Zooms

Cameras with zoom lenses give you a lot of creative freedom, because you can "zoom" from a wide field of view to a narrow one. You can show your family against a backdrop of the sweeping vista of the Grand Canyon, or zoom in to fill the frame with just their faces.

Wide Lens Setting

The wider lens settings (such as 24mm on an APS camera or 32mm on a 35mm camera)

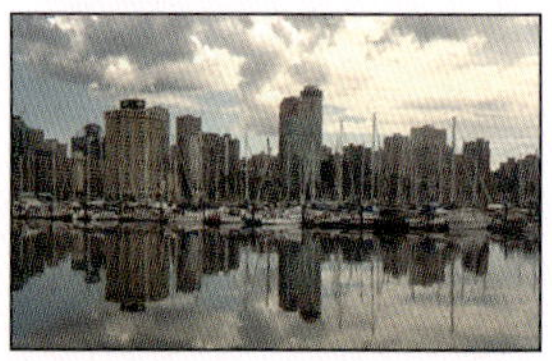

include a wide expanse of the scene in front of you, which is great for panoramas and group photos. However, this setting can cause distortion and is usually not good for close portraits.

Normal Lens Setting

In the mid-range is the "normal" setting, which closely mimics what the human eye sees (minus the peripheral vision). This is the most natural-looking setting, and as such, is not always the most exciting.

Telephoto Lens Setting

A lens setting in the 70mm to 140mm range (usually referred to as "tele" or "telephoto") magnifies the subject on the film to show more detail. Telephoto is the most complimentary lens setting for head-and-shoulder portraits. It's also good for cropping out unwanted distractions from the composition.

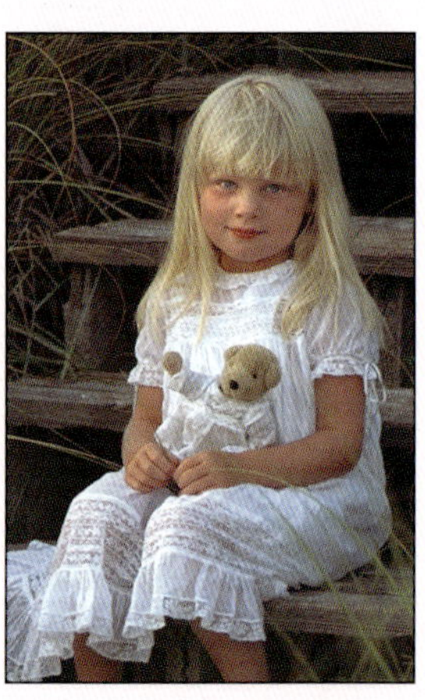

blur the background so it is less distracting, making your portrait subject stand out.

Flash Modes

Most point-and-shoot cameras offer auto flash mode, along with several other choices. These can include Flash Off, Fill-Flash, Slow-Sync or Night Flash and Red-Eye Reduction Flash. For more complete information on flash photography, see the section beginning on page 41.

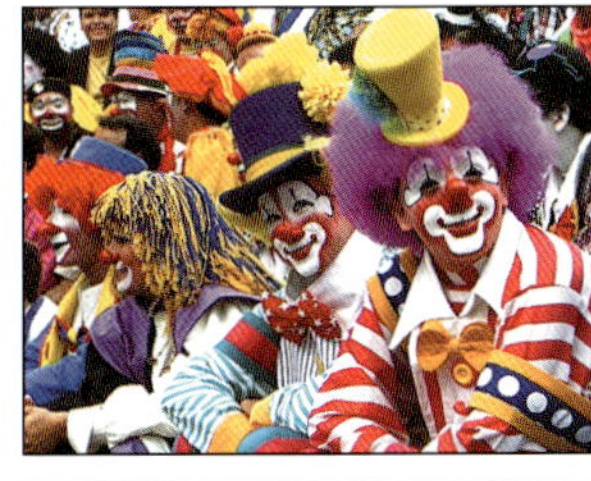

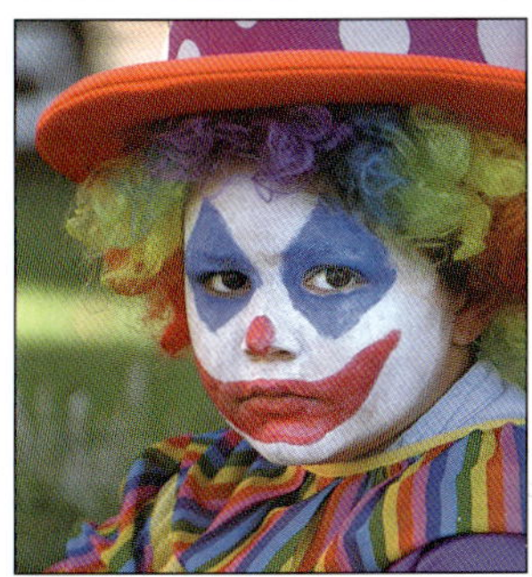

Normal exposure mode (top) captures the general scene. However, switching to portrait mode, and isolating one clown, puts the background out of focus and creates a less confusing picture.

Focus Lock

Most point-and-shoot cameras have a center-oriented autofocusing system. Whatever is in the center of the frame is what the camera will try and focus on. However, a centered subject is not always the best composition. There will be times that you want the camera to focus on an off-centered subject. This is the time to use your camera's focus-lock feature (usually initiated by pushing and holding the shutter release button halfway down). Simply center the subject in the camera's viewfinder, push the shutter release button halfway down and hold it, compose the photo so the subject is positioned properly in the frame, and then push the button down completely to take the picture.

The exceptions are one-time-use and focus-free or fixed-focus cameras. These cameras do not have autofocusing capabilities and are preset to a certain focusing point (usually six feet to infinity). If your pictures are out of focus with this type of camera, it usually means your subject is too close.

Infinity Lock

Once you understand the center-orientation of your camera's focusing system, you may find situations where you want to use Infinity Lock. This feature is available on a few high-end cameras and is useful if your subject is on the other side of a window, behind a fence or cage, or if there are foreground elements that may fool the autofocus system. Essentially, this function tells the camera to ignore the window or the nearby tree branches and set focus at infinity instead. See the sidebar in the Travel Photography section on page 79.

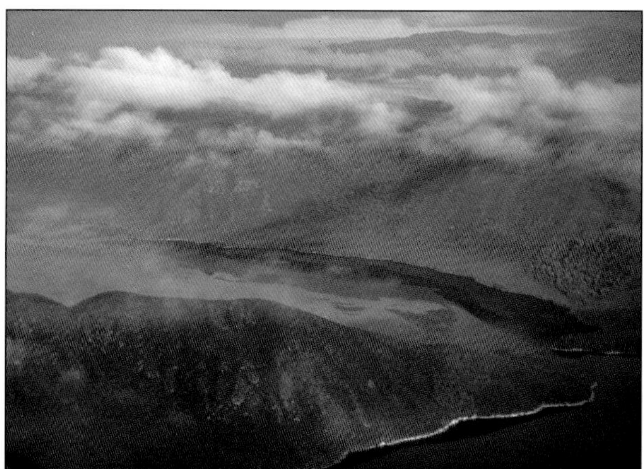

The Infinity Lock feature lets you take pictures out of airplane and other windows without confusing the camera into trying to focus on the glass instead of the scene outside.

Focus Features

Fixed-Focus or Focus-Free Cameras

These are generally the least expensive, because they do not have autofocusing capability. Instead, they are designed to produce adequate results as long as your subject is at least six feet or so away from your camera. One-time-use cameras are examples of fixed-focus cameras.

Autofocusing (AF) Cameras

An AF camera is far better, because it actually determines how far away the subject is from the camera. Lower-end AF cameras offer only two or three autofocusing zones, while the best can pinpoint the focus on your subject.

Underwater Capability

A few point-and-shoot cameras have underwater capability, usually down to about a maximum of 16 feet—plenty of depth for snorkeling and playing in the pool. An underwater casing can be purchased for a non-waterproof camera for similar underwater experiences.

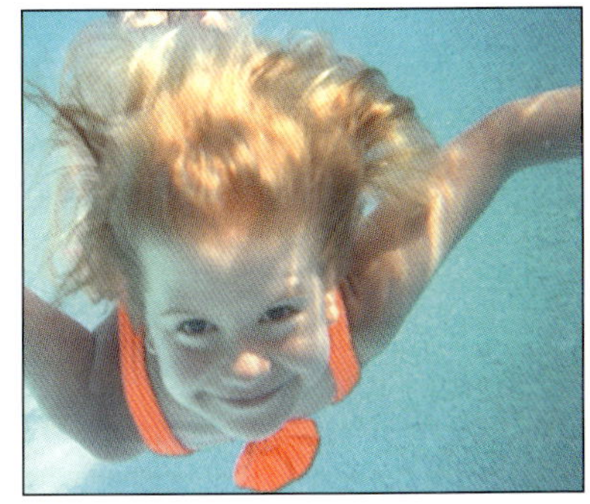

Film Speed (ISO) Settings

Some low-end cameras are very limited in what film speeds they will accept. Be wary of a camera that only reads films with speeds of ISO 100 to ISO 400. Today's ISO 800 speed films perform remarkably well, and there may be times you want to use them, such as for high speed action or in low-light situations.

Self-Timer

Self-timers allow you to delay taking a picture for about ten seconds, so that you can take your own picture or include yourself in a group photograph. The trick is finding something to hold the camera in the exact position that you want it.

Most middle- to high-end cameras offer self-timers, the nicest of which have an indicator light or a beep that quickens two seconds before exposure so everyone will be prepared with a smile.

APS Features

There are a few features most commonly found on Advanced Photo System (APS) cameras.

Back-Printing

With the back-printing function, you'll never again forget when a picture was taken. The top-of-the-line Advanced Photo System cameras can be programmed to print your choice of dozens of prepared captions or messages, as well as the date the photograph was taken.

Mid-Roll Rewind

Higher-end APS cameras allow you to remove a partially exposed film cassette, then reinsert it later and begin shooting right where you left off. This is a great advantage if you want to change film speeds (when moving from inside a house to outside, for example) or if you wanted to dedicate individual film cassettes to specific subjects.

Multiple Prints

If you know you're going to need extra copies of a special picture, some APS cameras let you decide on extra reprints at the time the picture is made. The camera records the reprint information invisibly on the magnetic layer, and the extra prints are made at the time of development. The idea is that it's cheaper and more efficient to make the reprints during the first run, than to go back for reprints later. But be careful! This is an automated function, so the photofinisher might make (and charge!) you for nine copies of a picture if you've programmed the camera that way.

Accessories

Tripod

Look for a small screw hole on the bottom of your camera. This is designed for mounting it to a tripod. Tripods are designed to hold your camera steady for low-light photography (such as a cityscape at night) or when using fine grain, slow speed films in dimmer light. They're also terrific for self-portraits, because you can compose the picture, push the self-timer and then dash into the place for the photo.

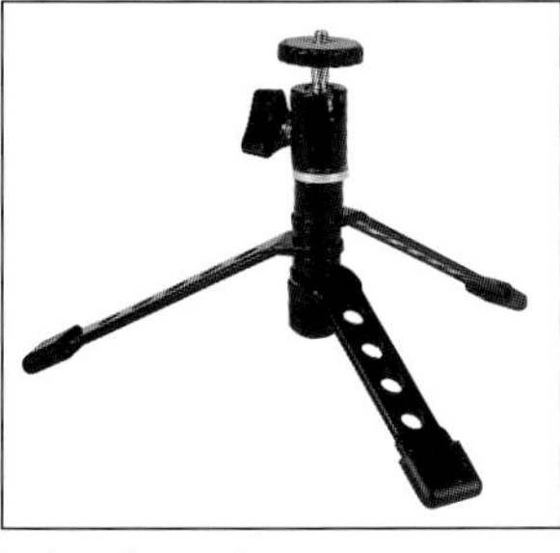

Unless you're planning to do advanced photography, there's no need to buy (and carry around) a full-size tripod. A tiny six-inch "pocket tripod" will fit into your camera bag or purse, and is adequate for most self-portraits, assuming you can find a steady surface (like a picnic table, fence, or rock) that is the right height to place it on.

Camera Bag

When selecting a camera bag, keep in mind that you'll usually want to carry more than *just* the camera. For starters, you should always have at least one extra roll of film. I carry an additional roll of my favorite film, plus film of a faster (or slower) speed, in case the lighting changes. And an extra battery is a must, especially if you're using the flash a lot. It always seems that batteries never die until you really, really need them!

Beyond these points, it becomes a question of personal preference. Do you want your camera bag to be your only bag? With room for items you'd normally carry in your purse or briefcase? Or do you want the camera bag or case to be able to slip inconspicuously into that same purse or briefcase? Many people enjoy a fanny pack type of bag for an active lifestyle. Others select handsome leather trimmed cases that are fashion accessories in and of themselves.

Most people however, end up purchasing more than one, so that they can interchange them depending on the occasion. The only important common denominator is that the bag or case provides adequate protection in terms of padding and keeping the elements out.

Remote Trigger

Some point-and-shoot cameras offer a remote shutter triggering device that lets you take the picture from a remote distance, without connection cords. Usually it either slips into a hidden compartment on the camera, or clips onto the camera strap.

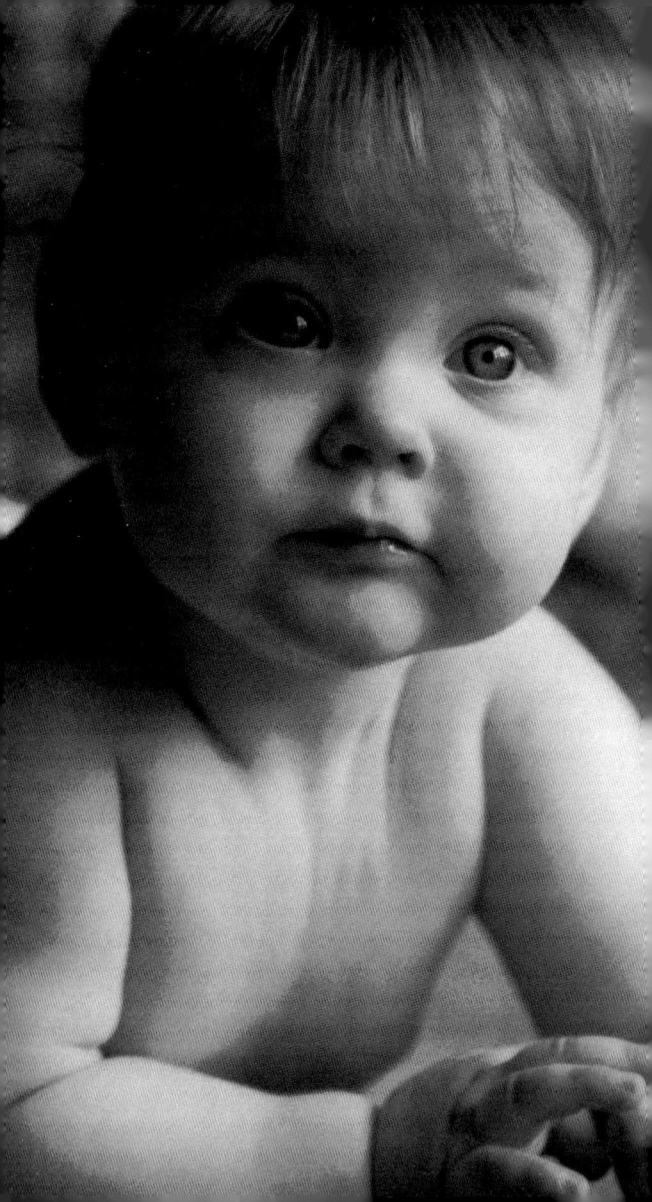

Understanding Film and Processing

Selecting the right film is one of the most misunderstood aspects of photography, but it doesn't need to be a mystery. The first step is to decide the type of film based on what kind of final product you want. For most people, this means color prints, so color print (sometimes called color negative) film is the product to use. For slides, select transparency film. If you want black-and-white prints, choose a black-and-white negative film. There are now several available that can be processed like color negative films.

Film Speed

The next choice is film speed. The higher the ISO number, the more sensitive the film, and therefore the dimmer the light can be for a successful photograph. But the lower the ISO number, the better the overall quality of the film and print (assuming you are using it in bright-enough light). Therefore, select your film speed carefully for the lighting conditions to get the best results.

ISO 100 or Slower Speed Films

Select ISO 100 speed films for general outdoor photography on sunny days, for enlargements, for portraiture, or when using a tripod. This speed of film has very fine grain, is very sharp and gives excellent color. When compared to other speed films in the same brand line, it offers the best overall quality (if you have bright enough conditions to use it!).

ISO 100 and slower films need to be used in bright sunlight or with flash. They yield poor results in dim or low-light situations, often causing underexposured or blurred pictures. (See the Troubleshooting section for information on blur and underexposure.)

200 Speed Films

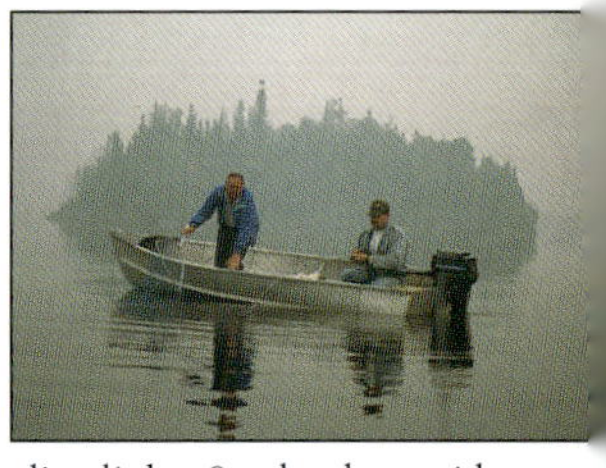

This film is a good choice for general shooting, cloudy days, indirect window light, for moving subjects, or when using flash. ISO 200 films require less light than ISO 100 for accurate exposure, allowing you to get better results in dim light. On the down side, you get slightly less quality than ISO 100 film in terms of grain and color but it is better in low-light conditions.

ISO 400 or Faster Speed Films

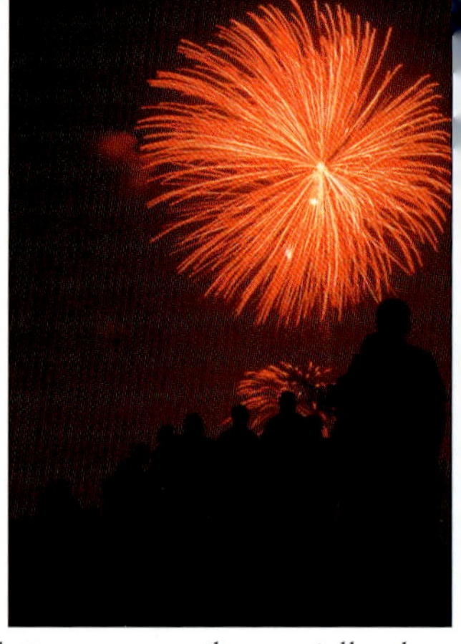

Select these films in low-light situations, when shooting indoors with flash, when using indirect window light, or with action subjects.

These films have the advantage of being faster than ISO 200 and ISO 100 film, giving you even better results indoors, at dusk or night, or when shooting sports. However, ISO 400, 800, and faster films are more expensive. They also tend to be "grainier" than 200 speed films, meaning they can look dotty or unsmooth, especially when enlarged. They usually offer less color saturation and contrast.

Processing

Always use quality processing. Quite often, photographers blame the camera or the film (or themselves!) when they get back images that just don't look great. You'd be surprised at how poor processing and printing can affect the final images.

See for Yourself

If you have doubts, try this test: take one of your negatives to the local photo store and have a reprint made. Then take it to the minilab in the mall. Then take it to a drug store lab, etc. And compare the results!

You'll probably get back prints that look very different from each other. One may look duller than the others; another may be too pink or too green; and another too dark or too light. You may even see one with white dust spots or scratches from unclean conditions. Stick with the lab that did the best job and the best service. They should do the job over if it isn't up to par.

Order Index Prints

When ordering my film processing, I always request Index prints. They are included with APS film, and many photofinishing labs can provide them for 35mm film as well. Index prints are miniature "thumbnail" pictures of every shot on the roll on one standard-sized print. The frame numbers show up in the corner, so there is no confusion. In one glance you can quickly find which photograph you want to reprint —no more trying to guess which negative is the one you want to print!

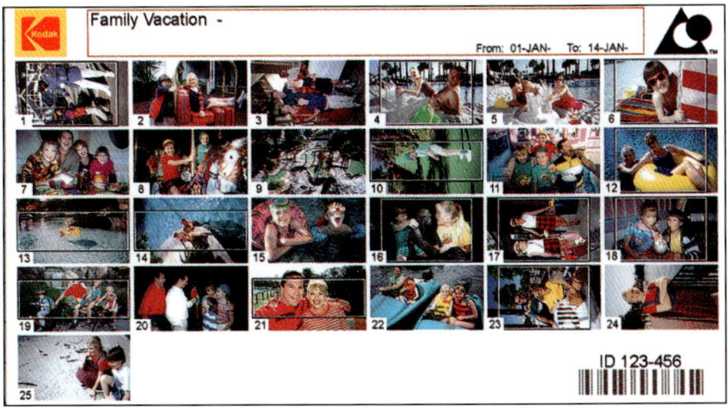

Index Print Comparisons

These three pictures are enlarged versions of what you might see on the index print for frame number 5 had you shot it in H-format (shown at top), Classic format (center), or Panoramic (bottom) print.

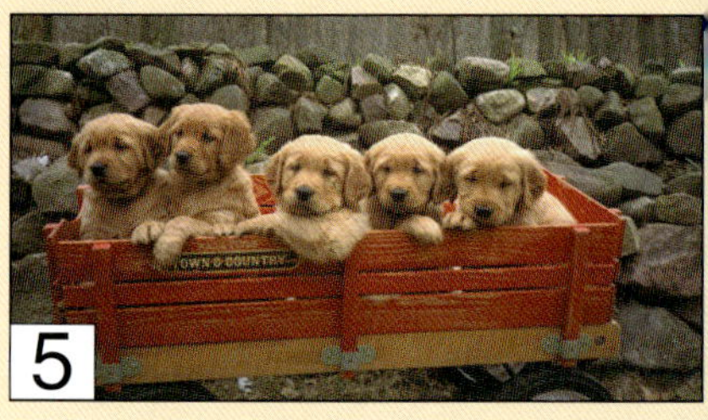

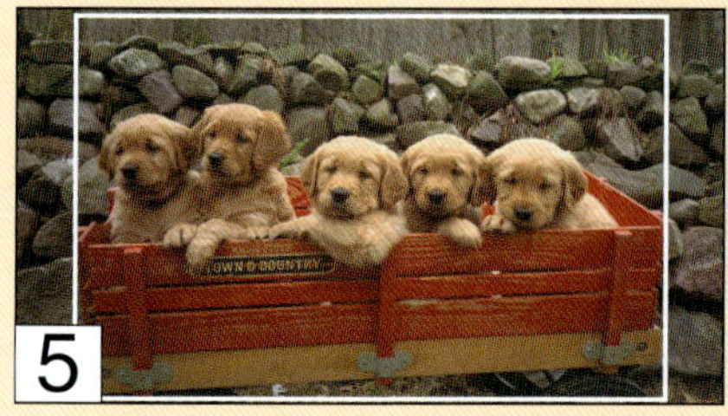

Note that the panoramic format trims off the top and bottom of the picture frame, and enlarges the remaining portion to a double-wide 4x10- or 4x12-inch size.

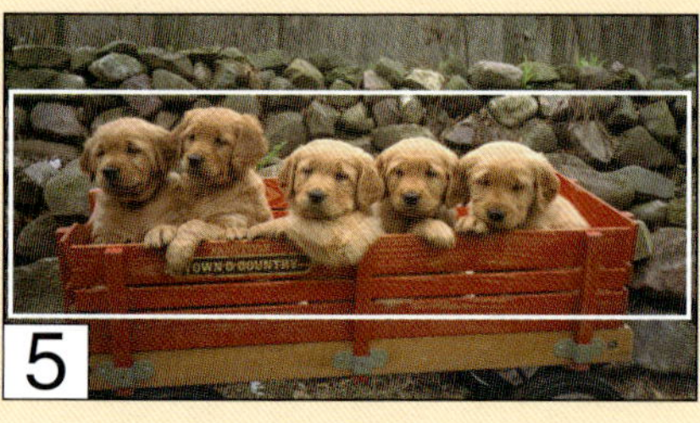

A big advantage of Advanced Photo System film and processing is that the cropping is a magnetic mark. Therefore, you can go back to the photo lab at a later date and select one of the other formats instead.

APS Print Formats

APS cameras usually offer a choice of three print formats, while some "panoramic" 35mm cameras offer two. Changing the print format is one of the quickest ways to alter the look of your photographs.

Standard 4x6 C-Format

Classic or C-format corresponds proportionately to the common 4x6- and 3-1/2 2x5-inch prints. The Classic-format print actually crops off a little bit of the image on both the left and right sides of APS film.

Wider 4x7 H-Format

H-format matches the shape of APS film, and prints are the closest to "full frame." They correspond in ratio to a 4x7-inch print.

Panoramic P-Format

Ultra-wide panoramics are most commonly printed to 4x10 inches in size. Selecting panoramic format is a quick way to turn many scenes into dramatic pictures.

Film Handling

- Always buy quality film, from a reputable seller.
- Buy fresh film (check the expiration date).
- Keep it in its protective canister until you're ready to use it (the container will keep it from getting humid and sticky, as well as dusty.
- Put exposed film back into the canister until you're ready to get it processed.
- Avoid getting the film hot—keep it out of the sun and don't store it in your car. Film that has been excessively heated can have nasty color shifts. This can occur in the box, or in the camera.
- If your film is cold from refrigeration or winter temperatures, warm it in your pocket inside the canister; this will cause condensation to accumulate on the outside of the container instead of on the film.
- Store your negatives in their sleeve (or in the APS film cassette) and keep them in a dry, cool area of your house.

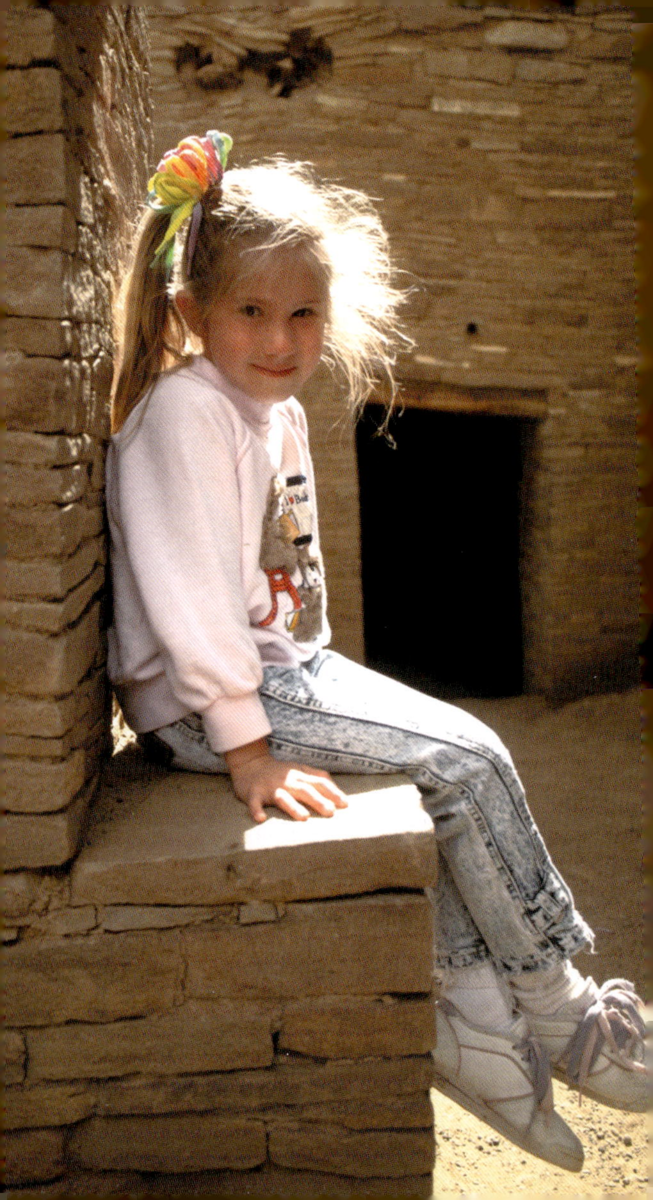

Lighting and Photography

Light is the single most important element in photography because it has such an important effect on how we see our subject. It can be soft and diffuse, or harsh with deep shadows. It can be natural, modified, or man-made. There are many ways that you can use lighting to affect the outcome of your photograph.

Bright Sunny Days

When it is sunny, colors look bright, and there is usually a wonderful blue sky in the background. It's great for bold landscape pictures, especially when you use the dark shadows for compositional impact.

When photographing people, the sun can cause harsh shadows on your subjects' faces, especially at noon when the sun is at a high angle. The usual recommendation is to shoot with your back to the sun and your subject facing into the sun. This can reduce some of the shadows, however it may also cause the subject to squint or frown. This wrinkling of the face looks exaggerated because of the harsh shadows.

As you and your subject rotate in relation to the sun, the eyes will fall into shadow (cast by the nose and eyebrows), eliminating squinting but obscuring the eyes. Not very flattering! Some solutions include:

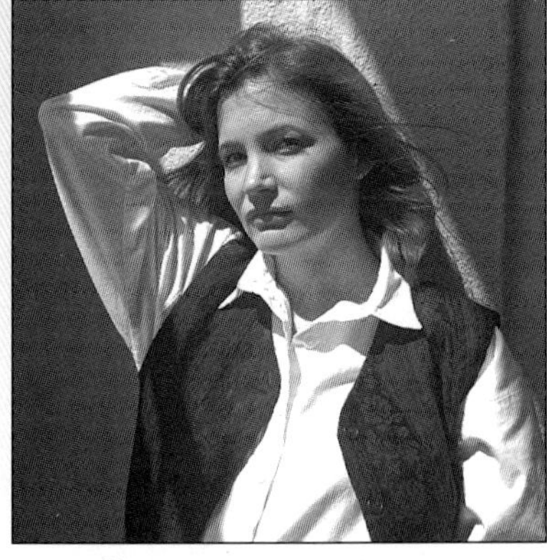

- Move into the shade.
- Wait for a cloud to pass overhead.
- Wait until the angle of the sun is lower (late afternoon or morning).

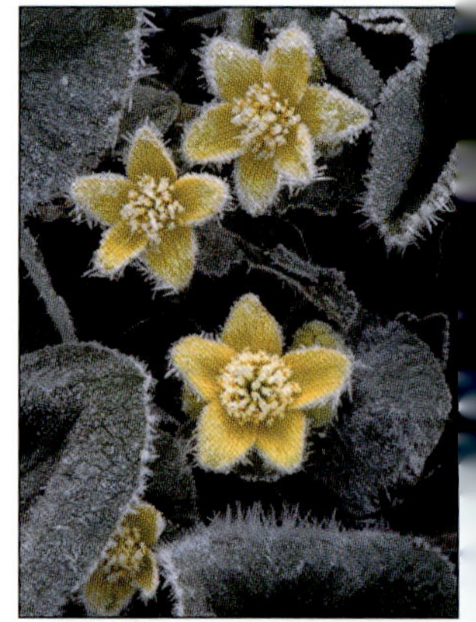

• Best yet, use fill-flash. (For more information on how fill-flash can reduce harsh shadows, see page 43.)

Overcast Days

This might not be the "best" weather you can imagine from an enjoyment point of view, but it's perfect for portraiture and flowers. Cloud cover diffuses the sunlight creating soft, complimentary lighting. You'll still see shadows, but they are minimal—just enough to show the contours of the face or flowers without emphasizing wrinkles or blemishes.

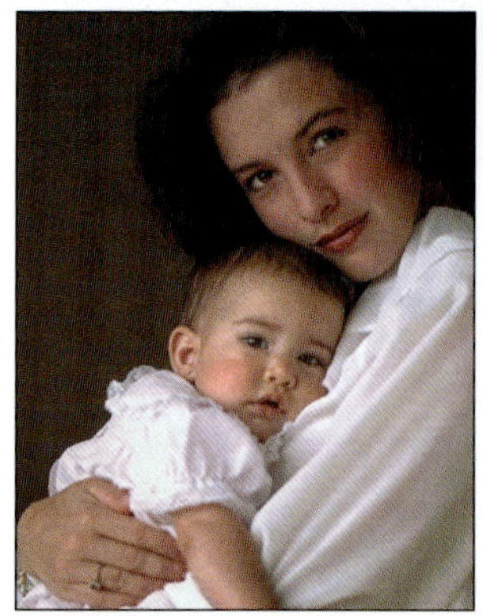

Northern Light

Long before the advent of electricity and electronic flash, the painting masters set up north facing studios so that their subjects were lit with flat, diffuse light from the windows. Diffuse lighting brings out the subtle contours of a person's face without casting harsh shadows or making the subject squint. Plus, you can shoot indoors regardless of the weather outside.

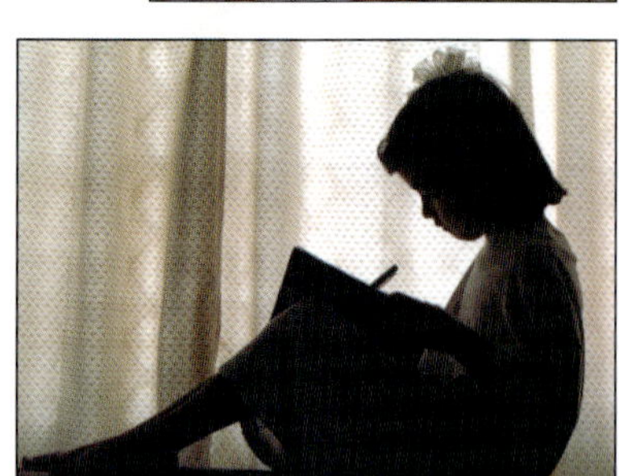

Backlighting

Most photography books tell you to avoid backlighting (where your subject is lit from behind). But, haven't you seen a magnificent silhouette shot at sunset? That's backlighting, after all! Successful backlit pictures depend on planning the affect you want to achieve.

The most important concept in backlighting is that the side of the subject that you can't see is all lit up, while you're looking at their dark, shadowed side. Below are a few ways to handle backlit situations.

Silhouettes

Silhouettes of people against the sky or bright backgrounds can be wonderful. The trick is to pose your subjects (or reposition yourself) so you can discern the form of their body. For example a profiled face

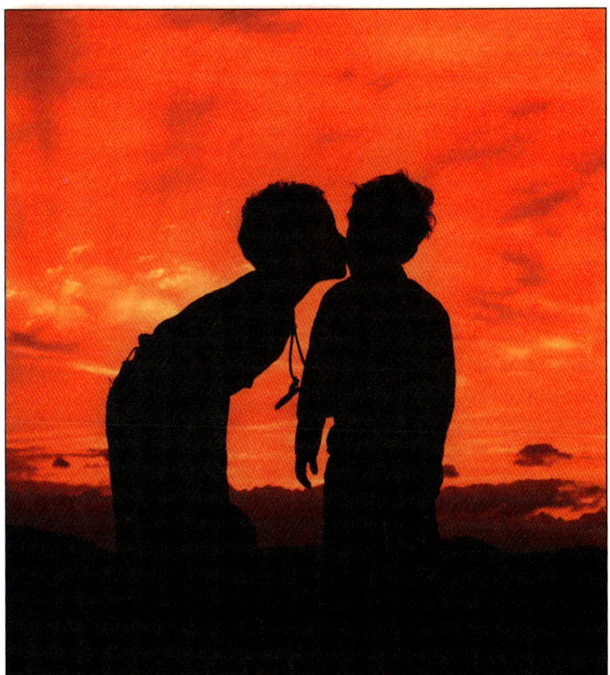

gives more information (the shape of the nose, chin, lips, etc.) than the silhouette of the back of a head.

Silhouettes with Flash

Try "popping" a silhouette with flash. You'll get the beautiful background, like the sunset, while the flash lights up the front of the subject. On many cameras, this can be achieved with Night Sync (sometimes called Slow-Sync) mode or Fill-Flash mode.

Translucency

Backlit photos of translucent objects tend to make them glow with color. This is especially effective with leaves and flower petals, as well as stained glass and fabrics.

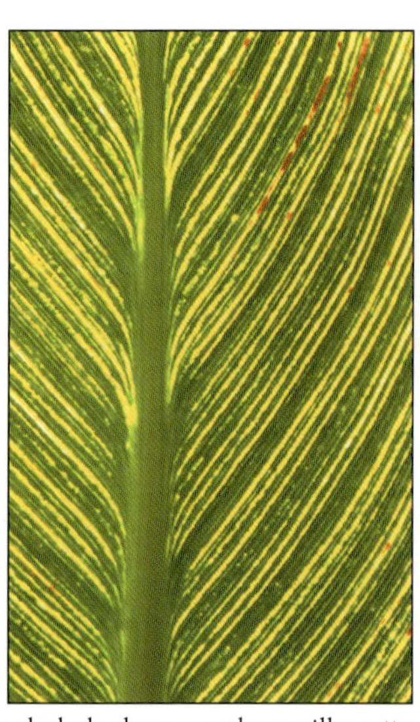

Rimlighting

Often you can use backlighting to highlight or rimlight the edge of your subject. Moving slightly to one side will show more of a "lit rim", forming a crescent moon of light on a person's head, for example. You may wish to add fill-flash so the front of the subject doesn't fall into dark shadows—unless a silhouette is the effect you're trying to achieve.

Photographing the Light Source

Many times, you may wish to include the light source itself in the picture. If it is extremely bright, like the sun at sunset, you will have a backlit situation. Often, however, the light may be a candle, streetlight or lighthouse that gives off relatively little light. If you use fast-speed film and steady the camera, you may create a very realistic photo of the scene, with the candle flame or other light source appearing "lit."

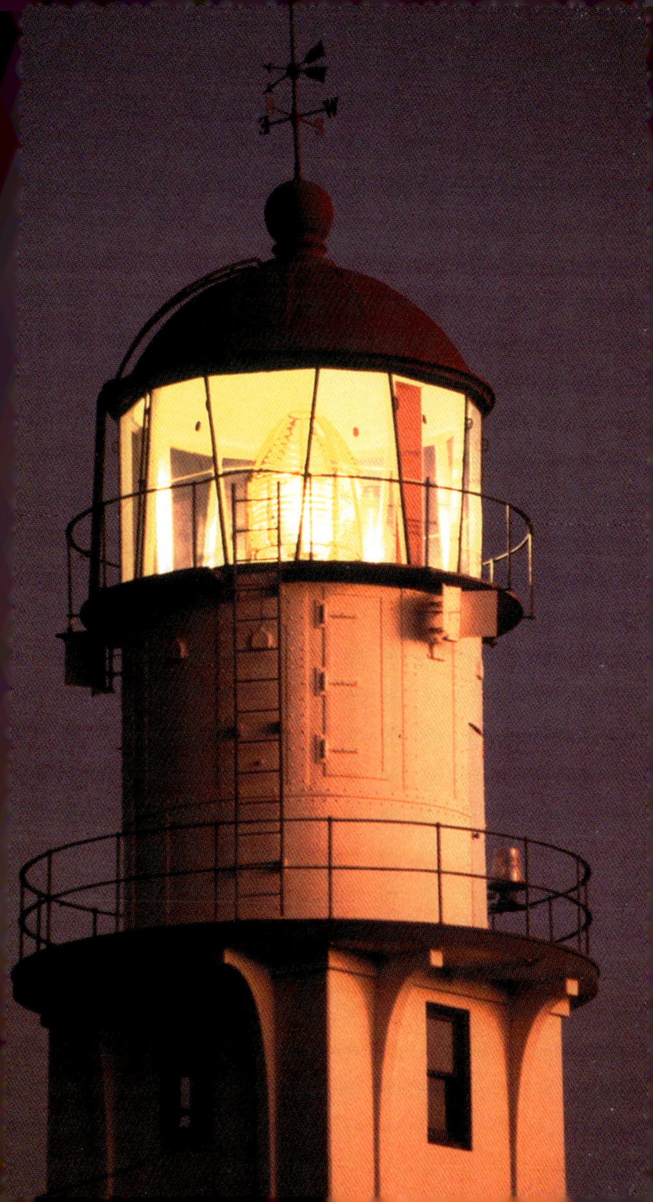

Flare

Flare is a common "problem" when you allow direct sunlight to hit the lens, because it can cause glare, light streaks, or lowered contrast in your pictures. Though hard to predict, these can sometimes cause happy accidents. However, in general, you'll want to try to shade the lens from direct sunlight.

The Color of Light

Many factors affect the color of light, but three will play a big part in your photographs.

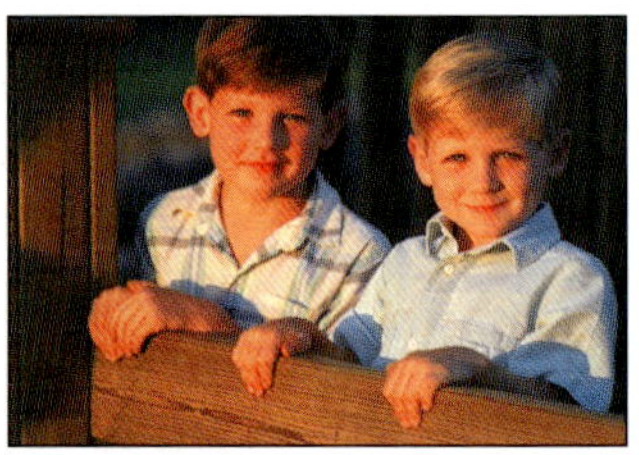

The warm glow of afternoon light creates pleasing portraits.

Time of Day

Late afternoon and early morning sunlight have a warm glow. The sunlight passes through more of the atmosphere at these times, than at high noon.

Color Balance

This book is not the place for a scientific discussion of the "color temperature" of different light sources, but you do need to know that most films are balanced to render "daylight" correctly. Most films are "daylight balanced" and deliver perfect color in typical midday sunlight. Move into the shadows and the light is cooler (bluer). Move indoors under tungsten or household bulbs, and the light appears warmer (more yellow and red). Flash is daylight balanced.

You can really see these color changes when you look at the pictures on the next page. The light of the sunset colors the scene vibrant red. In the snow scene at bottom, compare the color of the shadowed trees (blue) and the sunlit trees (yellow).

Pollution

Pollution, dust, and atmospheric debris can all add warmth to the light as well. This is why polluted cities often have the most spectacularly colored sunsets.

Flash Lighting

See the next chapter for a more thorough discussion of flash.

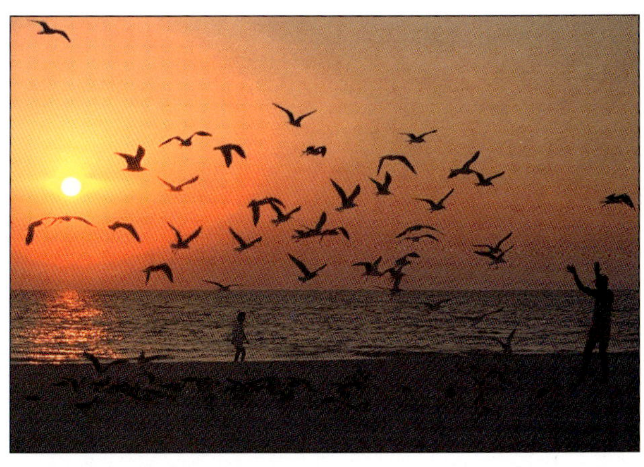

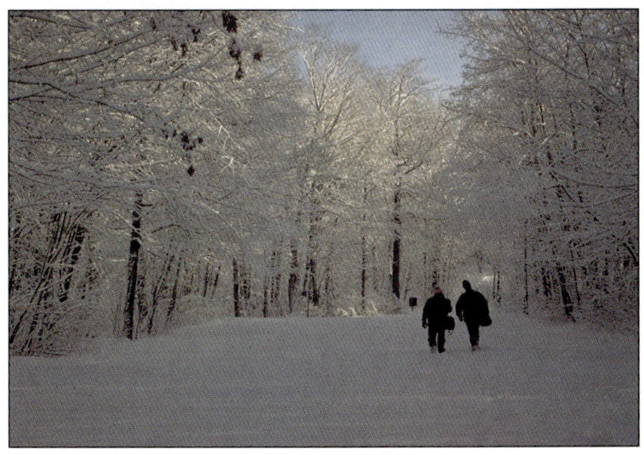

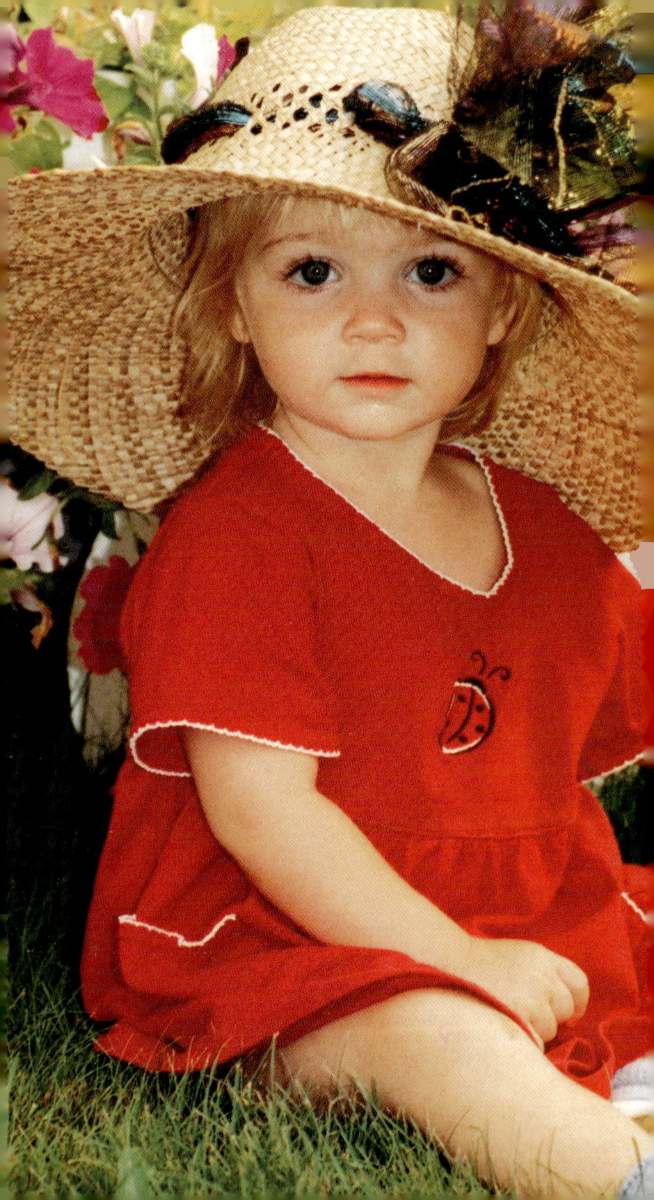

Using Your Camera's Flash

Most compact cameras have built-in flash units that will automatically fire in low-light conditions. Usually, the result will be a well-exposed subject and a dark background. Some high-end cameras will also fire if they detect a backlit situation, so your subject doesn't appear as a silhouette.

If your camera boasts multiple flash modes then you have some excellent creative tools to work with—and they are easier to use than you think once you understand their functions.

Going the Distance

Your camera's flash isn't going to light up Fenway Park or the stage at Rockefeller Center—but how many times have you seen the flashes pop when the star hitter comes to bat, or the heroine comes on stage?

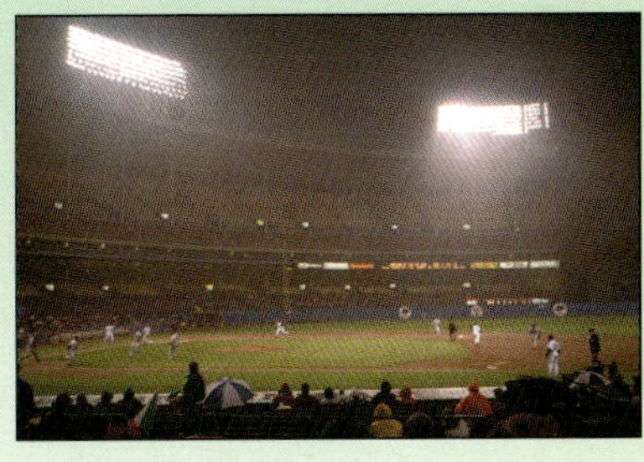

What is happening is that the camera recognizes that you are in a low light situation, so it *wants* to use auto-flash, even though the flash only has a reach of 6, 10 or maybe 20 feet. Less sophisticated cameras may drastically underexpose the image. At the very least, it drains the battery prematurely.

It's important to understand your camera's flash modes, as well as its effective flash range with the films you use (check your instruction manual). Armed with this knowledge, you can "out-think" the auto-flash, which probably only gives good results in "average situations" such as a subject who is standing 6 feet away.

Auto-Flash

Today's compact cameras have far more advanced auto-flash features than just a few years ago, but they still can't guess your creative aspirations. For example, a high-end camera may be able to detect a backlit situation and automatically send out a flash to help light up your subject's features. But what if you wanted a silhouette? Read your instruction manual carefully, to learn more about how (and when) your flash operates.

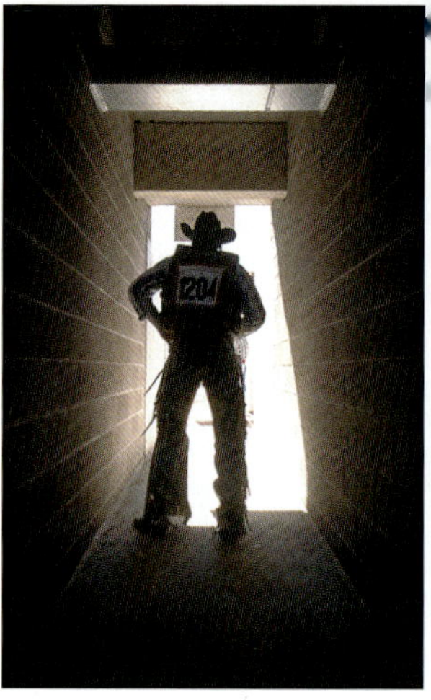

Red-Eye Reduction Flash

Unfortunately, red-eye reduction flash only reduces that annoying red-eye problem that some people seem prone to in pictures. It often crops up when taking flash pictures in dim light, especially if your subject has light colored eyes. It occurs when your subject's pupils are dilated and the flash is close to the camera's lens. (Therefore, cameras such as SLRs that have the flash far from the lens suffer less from this problem.)

Red-eye reduction flash works by emitting a pre-exposure light or series of flashes designed to narrow the subjects pupil size. If your camera doesn't have this function, or you find the pre-flash too annoying, you can achieve the same effect by brightening the room lights.

And notice the word "reduction" in the features name! These systems aren't guaranteed to eliminate the problem, but they do offer improvement.

Many computer programs now offer auto red-eye correction programs, so if you plan to convert your prints into digital picture files (or you shot with a digital point-and-shoot camera), red eye correction is now quite simple. You can use a special red-eye pen(sold at many camera stores and photofinishing labs) that neutralizes the red color when you dab a photo print with it.

Fill-Flash

If you learn nothing else from this book, learn how to use the fill-flash option on your camera. Fill-flash is one of the best inventions of modern cameras, because it greatly improves pictures in many different situations. For example, if you take a portrait on a bright sunny day, the sun casts harsh, unpleasant black shadows under the eyes and nose. It exaggerates wrinkles and blemishes and is generally unflattering light for your subject. By adding fill-flash, the picture looks basically the same, except the shadows are now filled and there are snappy highlights in your subject's eyes.

If your camera's flash system is reasonably good, rarely will fill-flash have an adverse effect on your pictures—so when in doubt, turn it on!

A little flash can do a lot for a picture. Bright sunlight causes harsh shadows; fill-flash fills in shadows with a small amount of light.

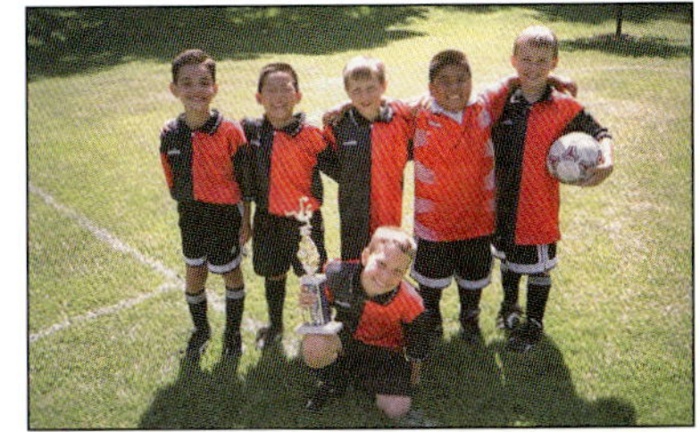

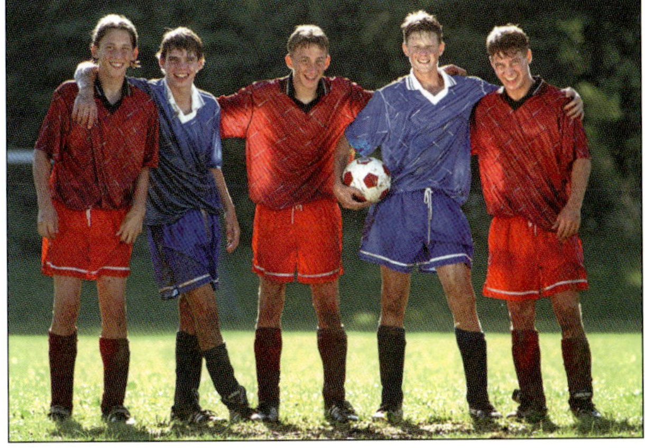

Black Background

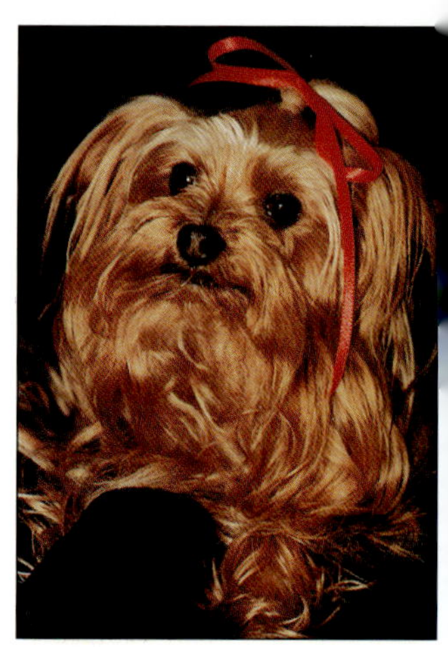

The typical flash picture outdoors or in a large room has a nicely lit subject and a dark background. This is because the light from the flash falls off quickly after illuminating the subject. It simply doesn't have the power to light up a distant wall or the Great Outdoors.

This black background can work to your advantage to accentuate your subject. Sometimes, however, it's nice to see more of the environment. In that case, try night flash.

Night Flash

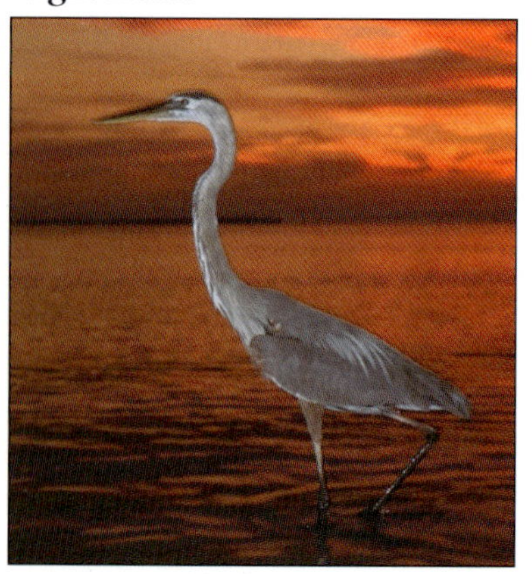

Night Flash Mode combines a flash exposure (which records the subject perfectly on film) with a longer shutter speed (which exposes the surrounding background as well). This allows you to mix those neon lights, room lights, or sunset sky with a well-exposed subject matter (instead of a backlit silhouette).

For optimum results, use high-speed film, such as ISO 400 or faster and hold the camera very steady. You can substitute fill-flash for night-flash if your camera doesn't have this mode, but the results may not be quite as good.

No Flash

Sometimes dim lighting can be wonderful by itself, such as at dawn or dusk. But your camera's computer says "not enough light." Overrule the computer's settings and select "Flash Off" (usually a circle and slash symbol through a lightning bolt). Then steady your camera with a tripod or against a stationary object to prevent blur from camera movement.

Most point-and-shoot camera flashes are effective up to about 20 feet maximum with ISO 200 film. This means if you're at a concert or a baseball stadium, turn your flash off! It can't possibly light the the performers or players; but the camera might think it did—leaving you with a drastically underexposed picture. Instead, plan ahead, load fast speed film; turn the flash off and steady your camera as best you can.

Similarly, some high-end point-and-shoot cameras can recognize backlit subjects and automatically pop the flash to fill in the details on the subject, in order to prevent a silhouette. But what if you want a silhouette? Perhaps you like the drama of a silhouette against a beautiful sunlit sky. The answer is to turn the flash off.

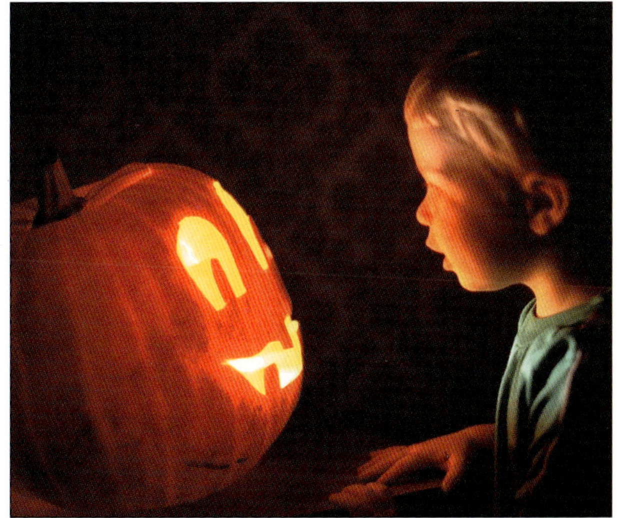

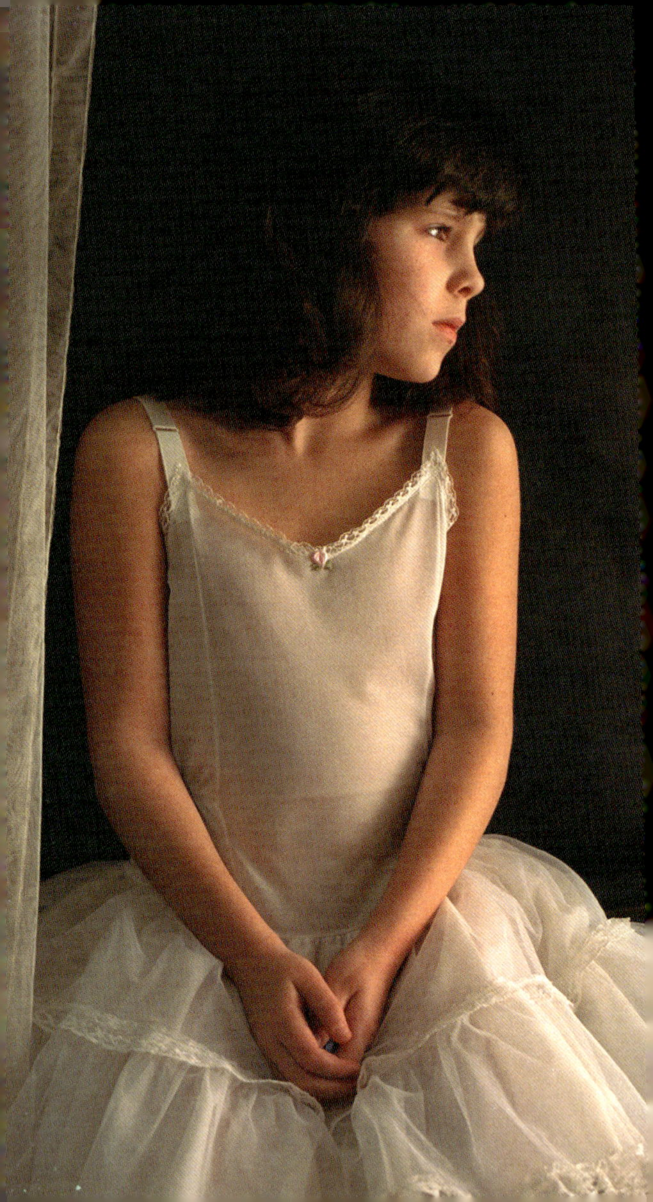

Better People Pictures

If you've ever seen a picture of yourself that you disliked, it's quite possible you can blame it on the photographer! There are definitely a few "tricks" you can use to make certain your photographs of people come out the very best.

The Eye-Level Rule

The number one way to improve most people pictures is to photograph them at eye-level. Most people pictures (and pet portraits) are best if you are shooting from the eye-level of your subject.

For toddlers, this means getting down on your knees. For a seated subject it means squatting down. For someone shorter than you, you should duck lower. And stand on something to shoot someone considerably taller.

The reason behind this rule is that when you're looking at an angle down or up at a person, there is usually some distortion—especially with wide-angle lenses. Your toddler, who is straining to look up at you, is not only in an awkward position, but his head looks huge and his feet look tiny.

The second reason is that a head-to-head eye level conversation tends to be very intimate. The same goes for an eye-level picture.

Test the theory if you don't believe me. In nine out of ten cases, you'll see a big improvement!

Breaking the #1 Rule

Of course, the eye level rule can be broken for creative purposes, to "shake things up." An extremely high, overhead angle can be unusual. Remember that "unusual" may be good or it may be bad—it all depends on your

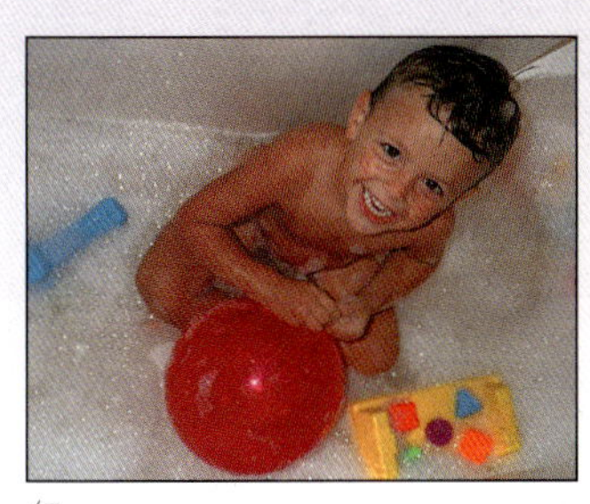

degree of artistry and the creative choices you make. We're used to looking down on kids and pets because we are taller. Switch it around, look up at them, and you'll suddenly have a very unusual picture.

People Are Vertical

People are taller than they are wide. Therefore, it makes sense that vertical compositions are more natural than horizontals. However, our cameras are designed to be held horizontally. It takes a little practice, but you need to become as adept at clicking the shutter on a sideways camera, as when holding it normally.

Practice in front of the mirror the first time, to make sure you're not covering any vital parts, such as the flash. And turn it so the flash is on the top, not the bottom, if possible. I had a camera once that took great pictures. But for some reason, whenever I turned it for verticals, my hand would cover the flash. And I wouldn't realize it until my finger got hot from the flash output—at which time it was too late and the picture was lost. Despite liking every other aspect of the camera, I knew I would lose too many vertical images, and I traded it for another model.

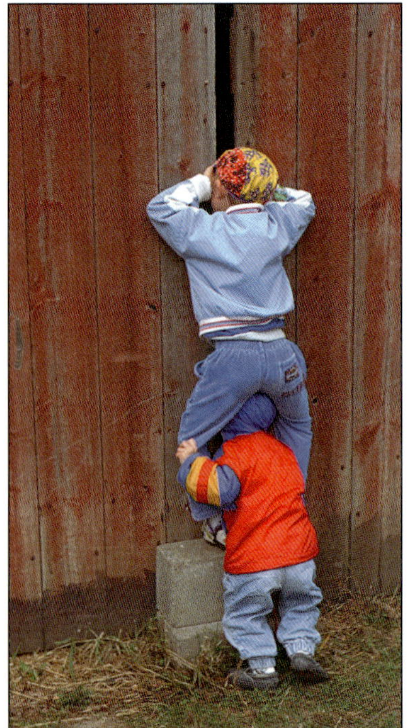

Note that the Rule of Thirds (see page 60) can apply equally well to horizontal and vertical compositions.

The Good Side

Head-and-shoulders portraits are the staple of the portraiture market. Just like a standing person, the head and shoulders are a vertical composition. Because no human being is symmetrical, every one has a "good side" (an angle that they look best at). The trick for the photographer is to figure out what that good side is, and then bring it out through composition, positioning and lighting.

Don't be afraid to walk in a circle around the subject. This achieves two things: 1) it helps change the background in comparison to the subject and 2) it shows your subject at 3/4, straight on in profile and even backside angles.

If you don't like the lighting because it is causing shadows on the face or making the subject squint, you can stay stationary, and they can pivot in a circle.

Often, there is a little dance, while you move a little and you ask your subject to move a little. It only takes a second or two, but the results can be a vast improvement.

The Overzealous Director

Beware of overdirecting. If your subject isn't fond of having his or her picture taken, a few minor changes in you position could seem like a delay lasting hours. This is especially true with youngsters, who can quickly tire of the "modeling" game. This is where digital cameras are so wonderful since you can share the results instantly. And if both photographer and subject aren't happy, you can erase the picture instantly, and take another. Likewise, if the results are good, your reticent model might become extremely enthusiastic.

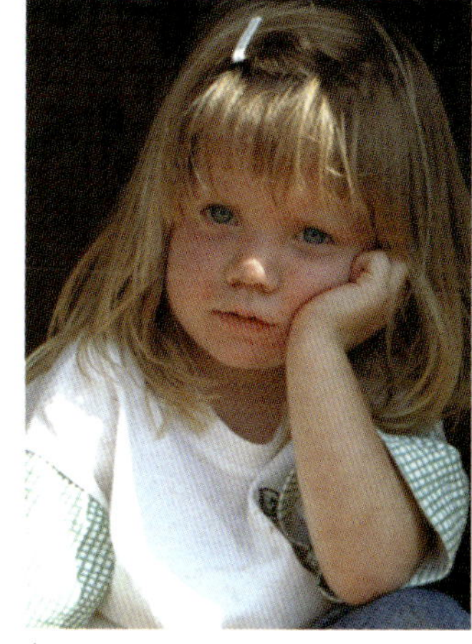

Groups

When photographing a group, take a minute to pose the picture. If you organize the people, you won't end up with a picture that looks like a police lineup. Think in terms of stacking or layering the people. Staircases are great for putting people at different heights so everyone's face is fully visible. Or try a front row of kneeling people with a sitting and/or standing row behind them. In addition, have everyone turn in towards the center of the group.

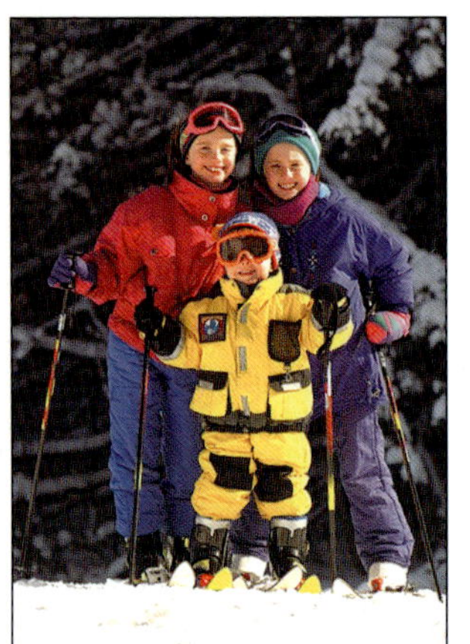

Candids

Don't beg your kids to smile for the camera or say "cheese," because even toddlers will quickly develop those forced-smile camera faces. It will make it hard to win genuine, relaxed smiles for your photos. Instead, use patience, have your camera ready, and wait for those spontaneous moments when the smiles happen naturally.

By carrying your camera with you on a regular basis and substituting candid photography for formal "line-up" picture-taking sessions, your kids will begin to see the camera as an everyday accessory. Consistently good candid photographs stem from your ability to put the subject at ease and be an inconspicuous and unobtrusive observer.

For great candid photos, watch your kids playing or working on an activity they enjoy. Compose the picture in the viewfinder and then give them a holler or greeting of encouragement. Usually, you'll be rewarded with a winning smile.

With kids, the eye-level rule mentioned earlier is especially important because of the size difference between adults and children. Crouching down and shooting at their eye-level is a good starting point for most of your pictures.

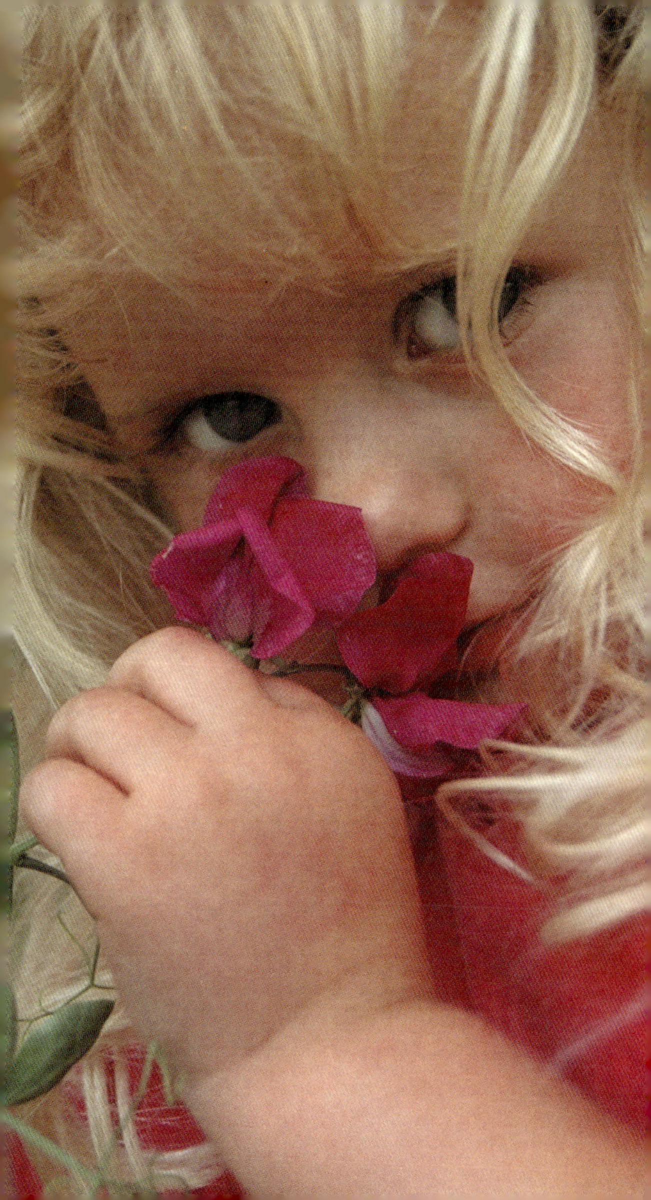

Interaction

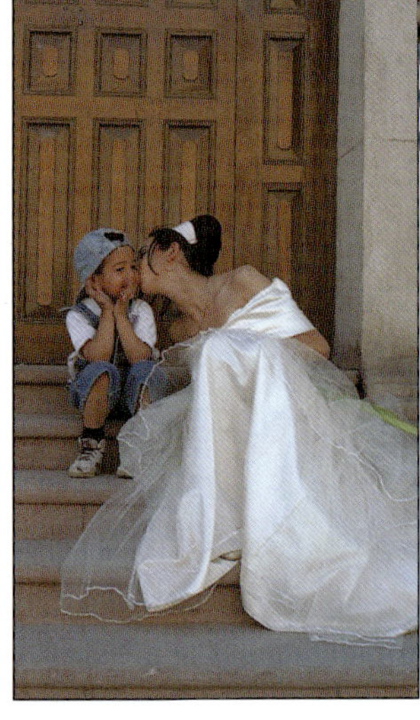

Some of the most successful photographs of people, and especially kids, is when you let them interact, either with their environment or other people or pets. Catching the moment when the bride gives her little cousin a peck on the cheek can be a priceless example of "interaction."

Photographing Humor

Creating or staging humor is actually easier, because you don't have to rely on chance. You do, however need creative ideas. If you want to create a humorous holiday card, for example, brainstorm with your family and friends. It might be as easy as costuming your kids as Christmas elves; or encouraging your kitten to climb the Christmas tree (again), but this time with your camera ready.

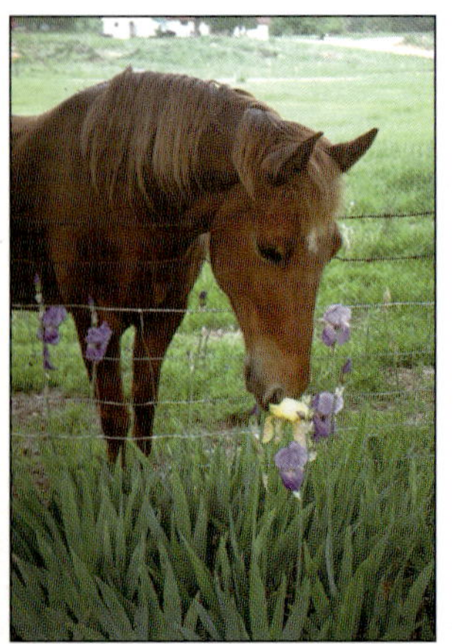

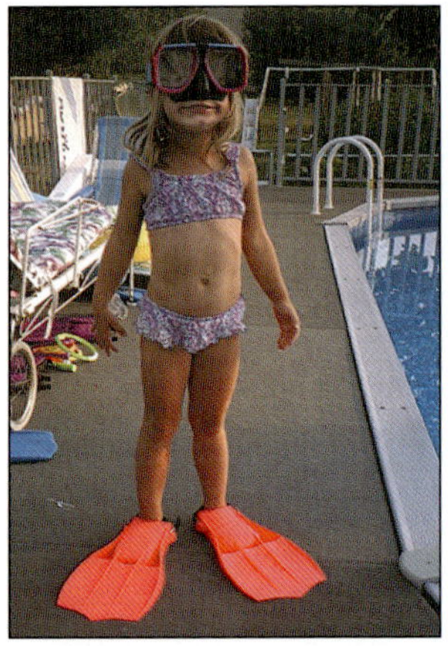

Finding humor requires an open mind, good spirits and quick reflexes. Humorous moments are fleeting. Knowing how to operate your camera will let you respond more quickly.

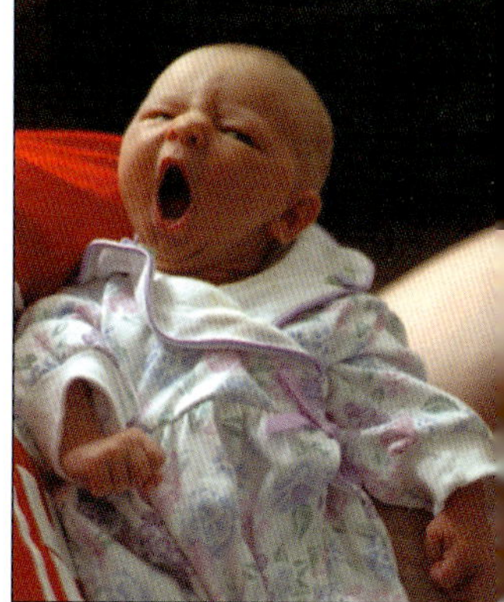

Tips for All Ages

As your children grow up, you may have to change your shooting strategy to get the best results. Here are a few general pointers.

Infants

Position your infant in a photogenic spot, surrounded by unpatterned, soft-colored blankets. The blankets will be a distraction if they are bright colors.

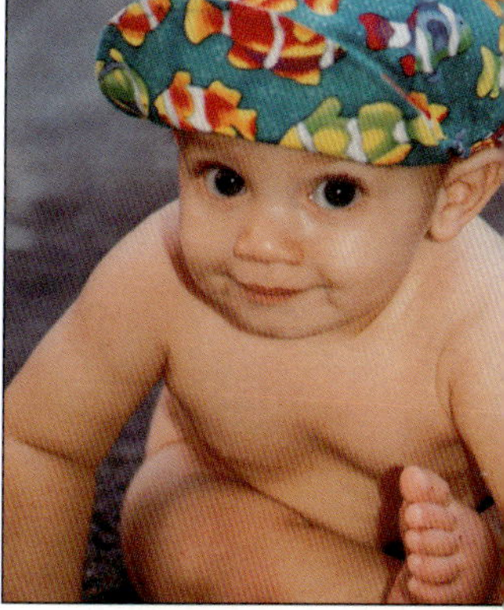

Position the baby near a window or use the flash. A car seat is a wonderful way to prop an infant up for pictures.

Get close or zoom the lens in to crop out unimportant background elements.

Wait for the expression you want, or try to prompt a smile or "funny face."

Toddlers

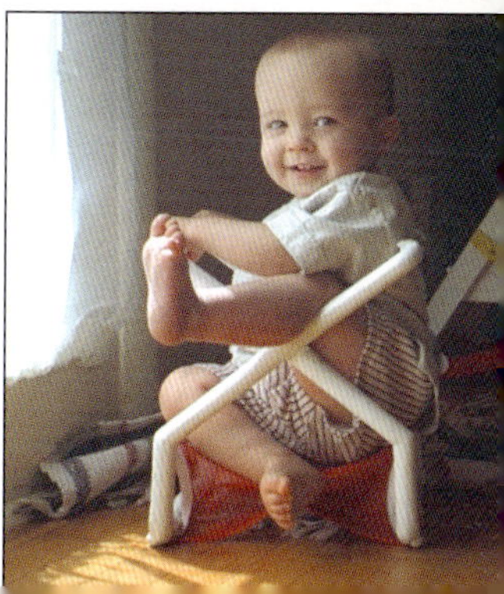

Toddler photography is akin to photographing Olympic sports, because your little subjects always seem to be on the move.

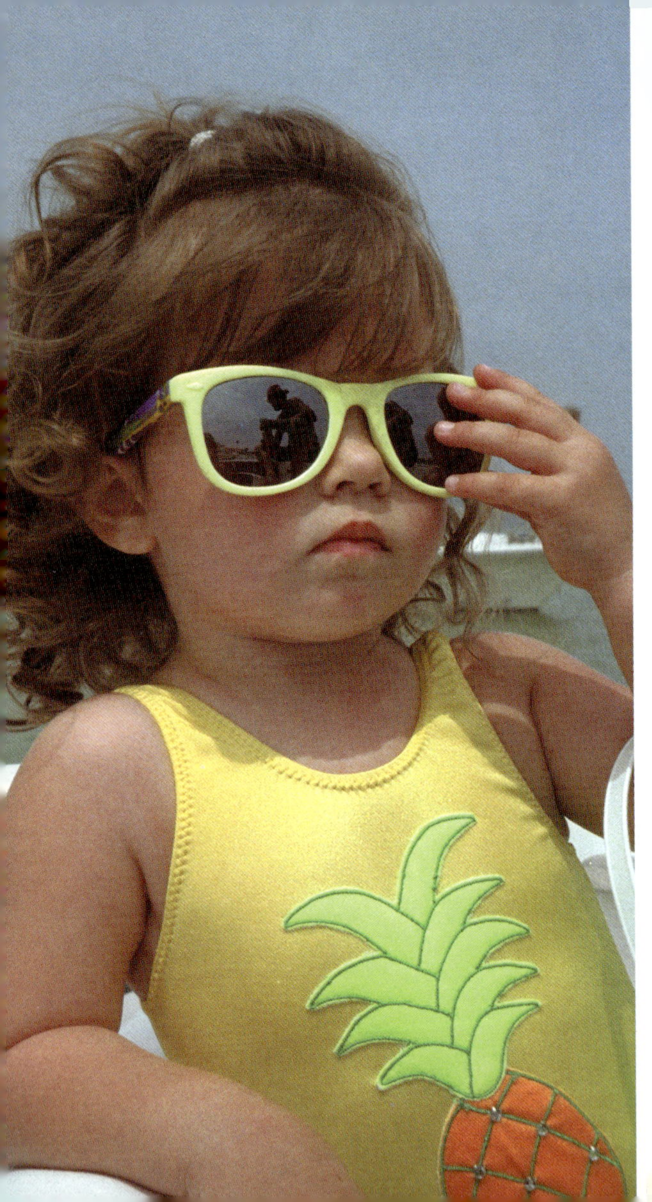

Your best chance is if you've practiced enough to intimately know your camera's setting and are therefore prepared to act quickly.

A good trick is to photograph toddlers when they're engrossed in an activity, like playing in the sand.

When toddlers see you pointing a camera at them, they'll usually come charging over to see what you're doing, making picture-taking next to impossible. Try to get them to forget about the camera by asking them to show you something (like a favorite toy) or perform an activity, like smelling the flowers.

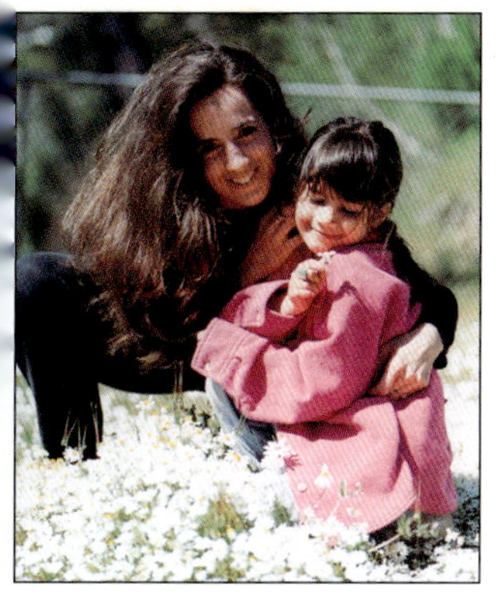

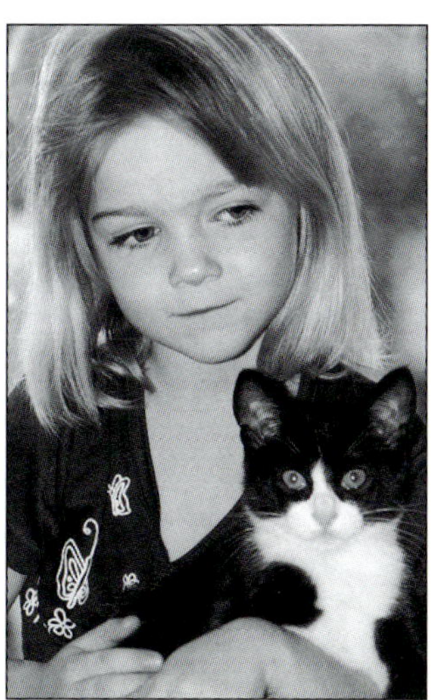

Preschoolers

Youngsters understand the concept of photography but are probably not overly self-conscious at this age. Avoid the "cheese" or "smile" commands, if you want genuine smiles, not phony camera smiles! Instead concentrate on candids. This is best done by pulling out the camera when they are engrossed in an activity, such as coloring, or cuddling the family cat.

Grades 1-6

Don't rely on school pictures as the only source of photos once your kids hit grade school. Photograph after-school activities, family fun, and holidays.

From this age on, it is especially important to take

photos of their friends as well; years from now they'll find great joy in seeing pictures of their childhood buddies.

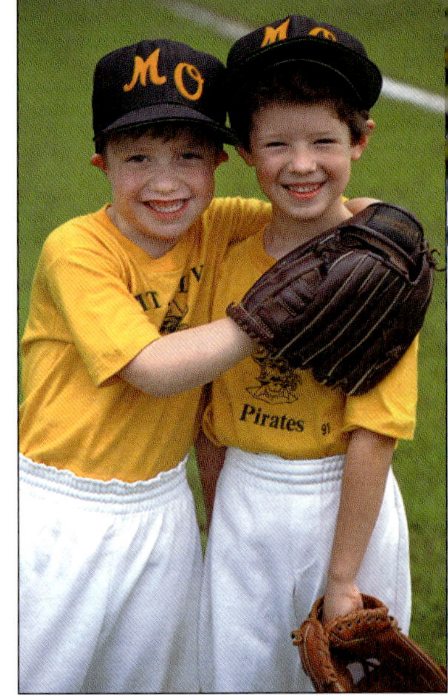

Tweens and Teenagers

Teenagers and "tweens" (the almost-teens) can be self-consciousness or rebellious about photography. If you've started early and made photography a painless and fun tradition, you'll minimize potential flash points.

At this age, kids may enjoy being the photographer, and encourage it by giving the child single-use cameras or an inexpensive point-and-shoot. Responsible preteens and teens will have no problem handling and taking care of the family camera, as well as working on a "film budget" to save up for a camera of their own.

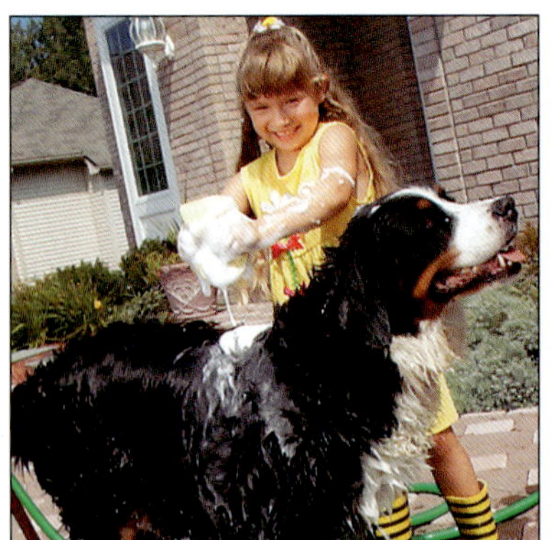

Another option is to invest in a digital camera. Your kids can learn, play, and work at photography to their heart's content without the worry of film or processing costs. (Though you may need to put supplies for a printer on the allowance budget!)

Photographing Your Pets

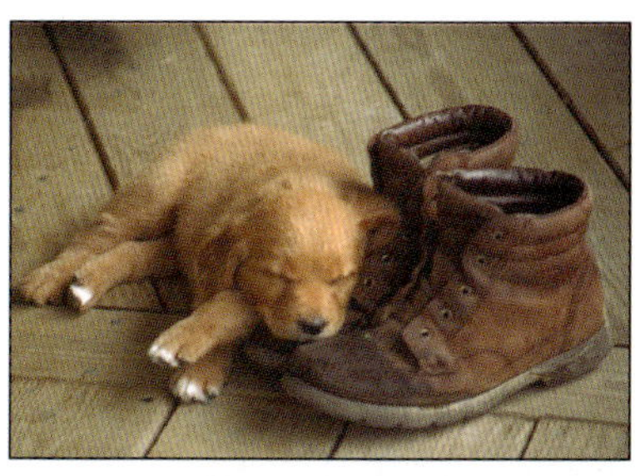

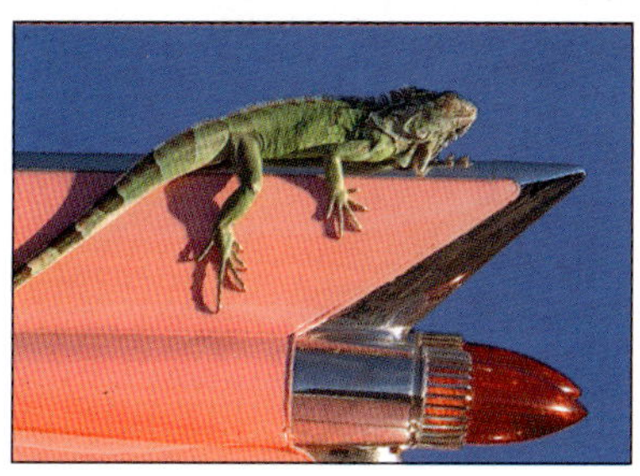

How many times have you heard that "pets are people too?" It's no wonder good pet photography follows the same principles as people photography.

"It's all in the eyes" might be a worn out cliche, but it really makes a huge difference. Just like when taking portraits of kids, you want to concentrate on your pet's eyes. First start by getting down to your subject's eye-level. Since you probably are taller than the animal, kneel or lie down. If the pet is small, it can sit on a window sill, a person's lap, or perch on a shoulder.

You may want to try and get them to make eye contact with you. If they're scared of the camera, frame the picture, hold the camera steady and then peek your eyes above the camera to make eye contact. If you're careful to hold the camera steady, the picture will still be well-framed. You can also get their attention by calling their name, clicking your tongue or squeaking a favorite toy—but be careful not to be too interesting you they'll come bounding over in response.

If you're photographing a person and their pet, you have two good portraiture choices: eye contact with the camera (from both subjects, if possible) or eye contact between the pet and its owner, showing their bond.

Red-eye is not just a problem with flash pictures of people, but it can also occur in pets. See page 42 for hints on avoiding red-eye.

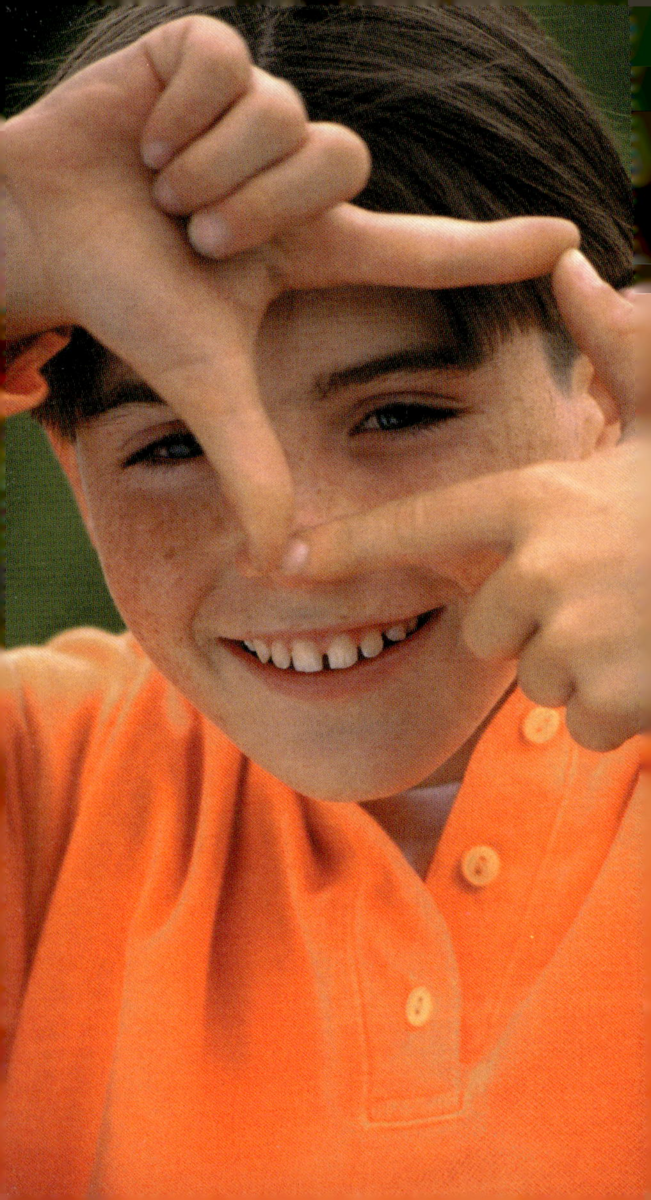

Photographic Composition

We all know the cliché of the movie director who makes a square out of his fingers to visualize a scene. Well, it might be a cliché, but it works. If you take a minute to think about your picture before you click the shutter, you will get better results.

No, you don't need to run around playing Hollywood. Simply take a good look through your camera's viewfinder. What's your subject? What else is important in the picture? If you have a clear idea about what you want to feature in a photograph, you can work to eliminate everything else.

Off-Center Subject

The bull's-eye method of composition is rarely the best choice. A more successful method is to put your main subject off-center. Most cameras, however, work against you because they orient the focusing system on the center of the viewfinder. Instead, place the main subject off-center, use the Focus-Lock feature to lock in focus and exposure on the subject (which is usually done by pushing the shutter halfway down). Then "shift" the camera (still holding the button halfway down) until you are recomposed. It may seem cumbersome and time-consuming the first few times you do it, but it will quickly become second nature.

Rule of Thirds

There is a simple guideline called the "Rule of Thirds" that helps photographers avoid the bull's-eye syndrome mentioned above. It applies equally to photography, painting, and other graphic art forms. The basic premise is to divide the scene into thirds and position the subject and other important compositional elements at these division points.

Begin by imagining a tic-tac-toe board superimposed over your viewfinder. The horizontal lines divide the frame into three equal horizontal sections, and the vertical lines divide it into three equal vertical

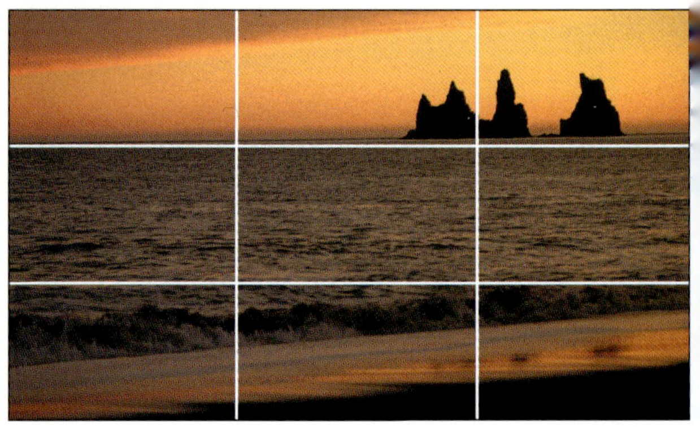

sections. Your goal is to then place significant picture elements (like your subject or the horizon) along these lines and especially at the points of intersection. Note that since this tic-tac-toe board divides the picture evenly, its shape changes for the different picture formats.

You can control the placement of important picture elements through your camera angle, the amount you zoom in or out, and your distance from the subject. As you become more accomplished as a photographer, you will soon start instinctually composing your images using the Rule of Thirds (or even more extreme off-centered compositions). But remember, like all rules, the Rule of Thirds is just a suggestion or guideline.

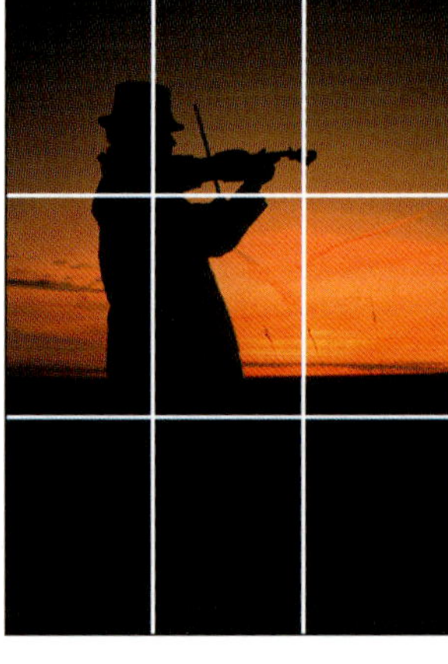

Imagine the scene in the camera's viewfinder divided into nine equal sections. Then position your subject along these division lines or at the intersection points.

The Horizon Line

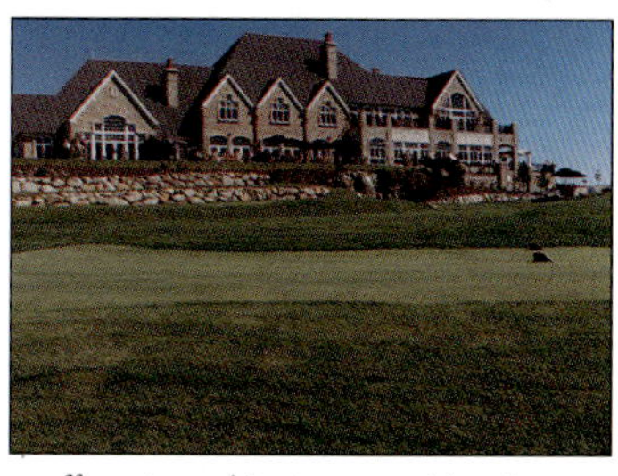

A horizon line (where the sky meets the land, buildings or water) is an important compositional element. Try to keep it level in your picture. Think of the Rule of Thirds and keep the horizon from spliting the photo in half. Just as off-center subject composition is usually best, so is an off-center (but straight) horizon line.

Using Leading Lines

In addition to horizon lines, the world around you is filled with other types of compositional lines—fences, window frames, rooflines, trees, or roads winding into the distance. The trick is to distinguish between good lines and bad lines. Bad lines are distracting lines, such as a pole "sprouting" out of your subject's head or a branch casting a shadow across someone's face. Good lines draw your eye into the photograph or make the overall composition more dynamic. These lines are usually diagonal or curvilinear, and should direct your attention towards the subject.

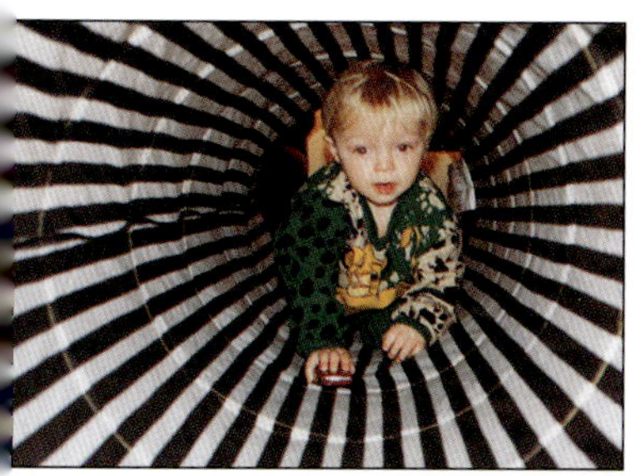

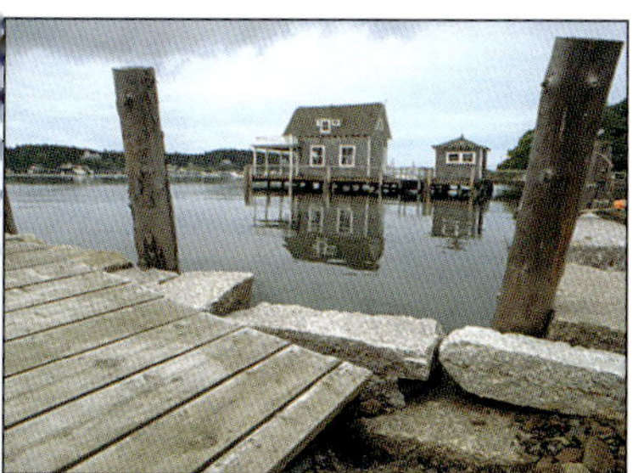

Room to Move

Active subjects need "room to move" in a photograph. If you are taking a picture of a person jogging from the left towards the right, they should be positioned on the left-hand side of the frame, so they are running into the space from the left. If you don't do this, the picture will feel cramped and crowded. This goes for the direction of your subject's gaze as well. This is because it is implied movement, and because it's human nature to want to "see" what the other person is looking at.

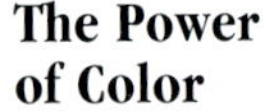

The Power of Color

Everyone is drawn to bright colors, and they can make or break your photograph. Our eye will naturally pick out bright colors, like

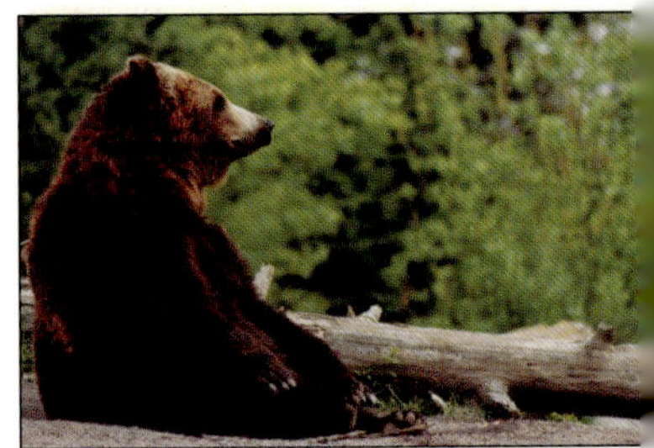

Your subject should be moving into or looking into the picture.

Try not to photograph your subject running out of the frame.

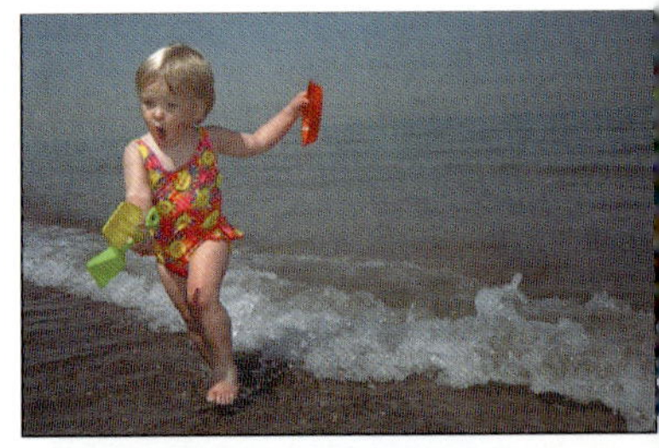

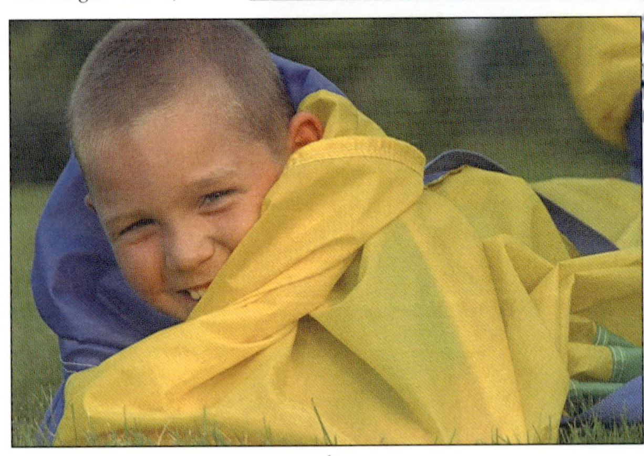

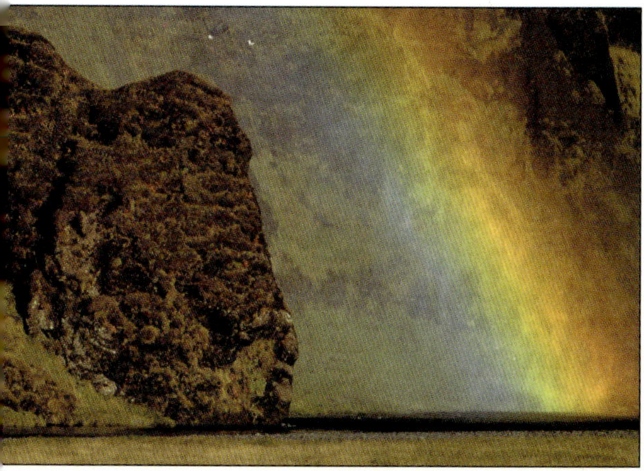

reds and yellows. These colors can be used to draw attention to important parts of the image For example, we might wish to draw the viewer's eye to the yellow flower in a girl's hand. Or to highlight a woman's face in a portrait by wrapping it in a bright scarf. But beware! Careless use of bright color can have an adverse effect. For example, a bright red sign in the background can be distracting if it draws your attention away from the subject.

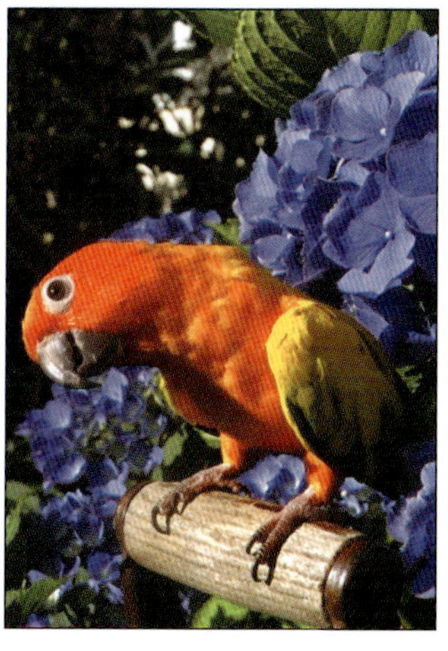

Colorful Moods

Many colors are also consciously and subconsciously associated with certain moods and feelings. For example, most of us think blues feel cool and calming; reds and yellows seem warm and exciting.

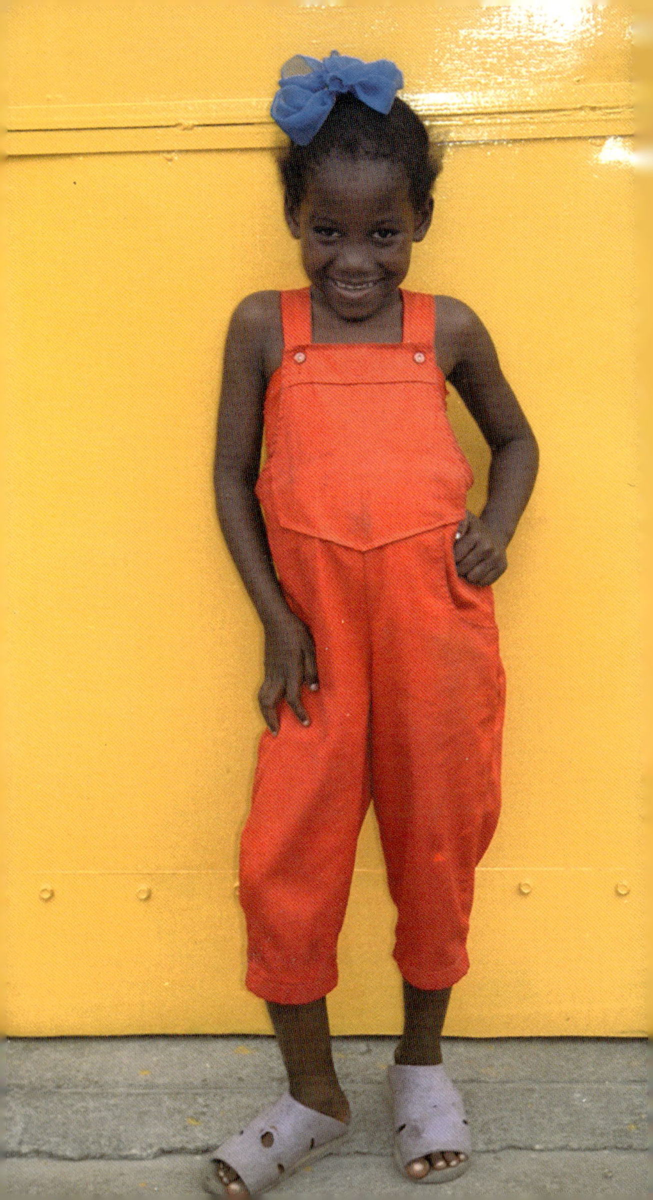

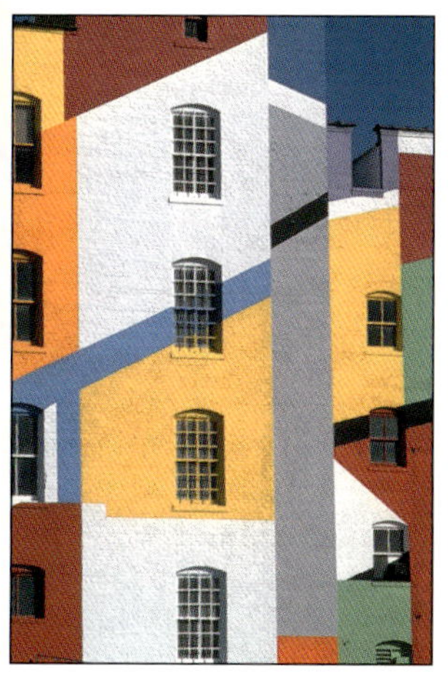

Give careful thought to the overall color scheme in a photo, especially portraits. Chose the clothes, props, and backgrounds carefully.

Color Hunt

When on a "photo expedition," many advanced photographers look for colorful subjects, because they are aware of the power of color. If they're shooting on a cold and overcast day, they may look for subjects that fit this cool, quiet mood. Or on a brighter day, if they see a great red flower, they may choose to make it the main subject, or start looking for another subject that the flower can accent.

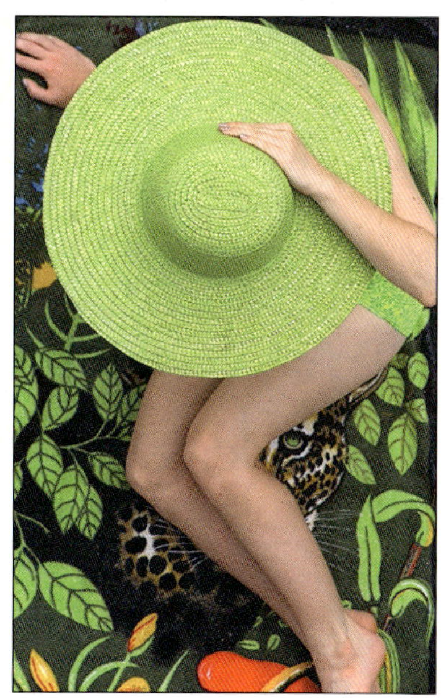

The trick is not to be overwhelmed by color itself—you still have to create a picture that works. Remember to think about what caught your interest before you shoot.

Changing Perspective

There is a lot of confusion (even with professional photographers) about the difference between "zooming in" on a subject and stepping closer. These two actions achieve VERY different effects.

Zooming

Zooming your lens (or changing focal lengths) merely changes the cropping of your picture, so long as you don't move in relation to the subject. Note the examples shown here. I started with a wide view of the scene (Picture One) and then zoomed in so that the subject appeared to get closer (Picture Two). Note that there was no change of perspective at all. In fact, the center section of Picture One is very similar to Picture Two, as seen in the overlay.

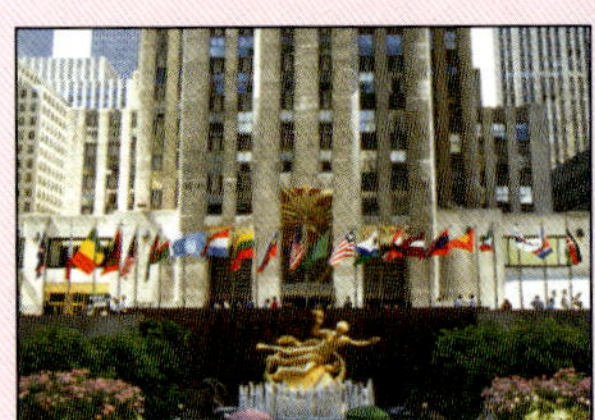

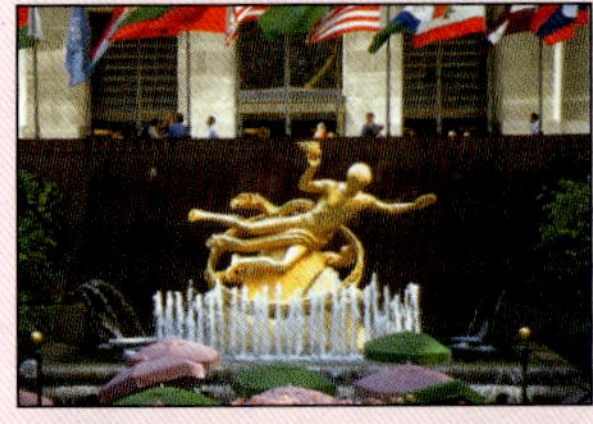

We could, of course, enlarge the tiny center section of the first photo until it was 4x6 inches. Unfortunately the quality would suffer because it would be such an extreme enlargement. Therefore, it is always better to "enlarge it in-camera" by zooming or changing the lens.

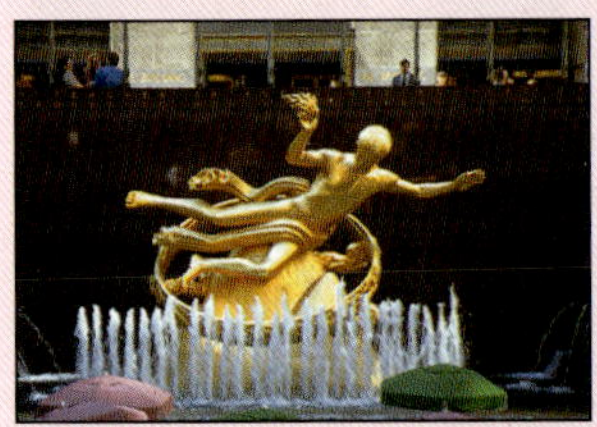

The ability to zoom your camera's lens gives you a lot more control over your final composition.

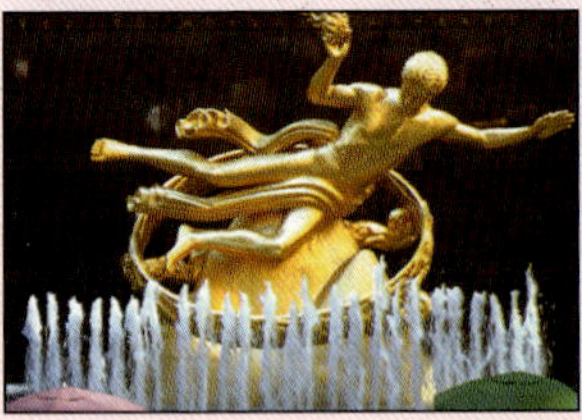

Stepping Closer

Changing the distance between your subject and yourself will change the perspective of the image. For example if you start with a full body picture with a wide-angle lens, and then step closer until you have a head shot, there are a lot of changes in the photograph. First of all, the background may seem different because you have changed the relationship of camera to subject to background distances. Also, wide-angle distortions become much more obvious.

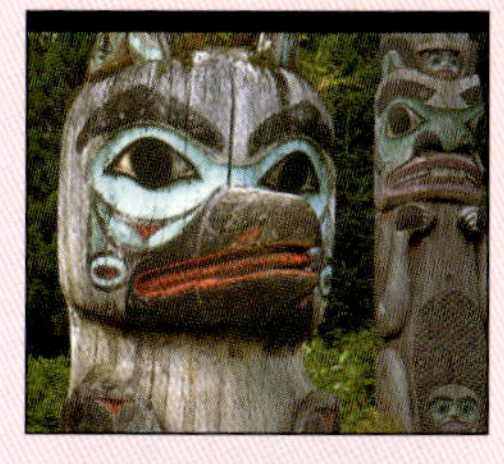

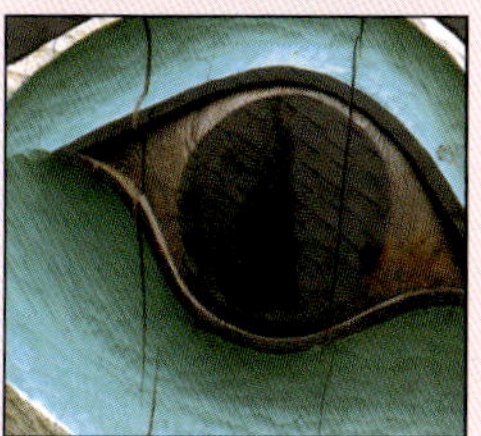

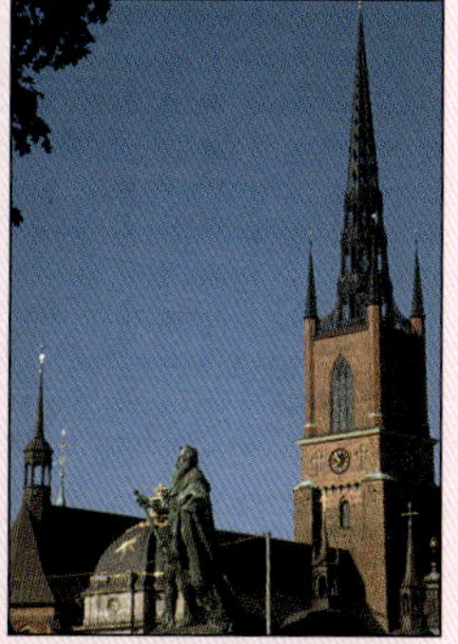

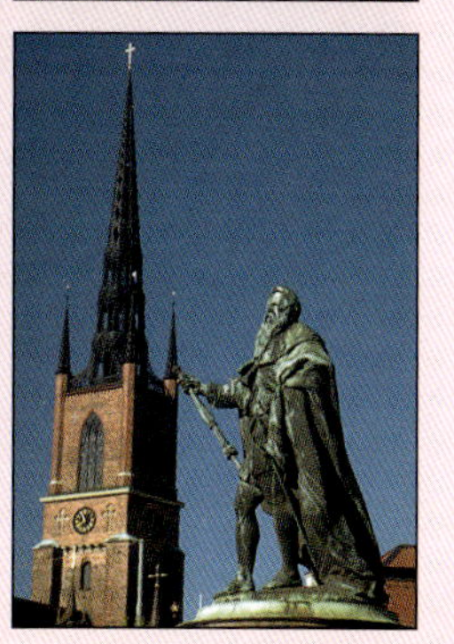

Changing Angles

Changing your angle can have drastic affects on your photograph, for better or for worse. By dropping low or moving high, you can often eliminate or hide unwanted background elements. If you're not paying attention, you can just as likely add them as well!

Here's an example: You're shooting a statue in the foreground with a church steeple in the background, you can exaggerate the size of one in relation to the other by changing your camera position. By moving in close to the statue and setting your lens on wide-angle, the steeple will look smaller (in relation to the staue) than if you had stepped farther away and used the telephoto setting.

Zoom in Now

Before you click the shutter, look at the outer edges of the picture. Do you see things there that you don't want to in the picture? Is there stuff you don't need? Is the background unimportant or distracting ? Try zooming your lens to get closer—and then closer still! Your results will be terrific.

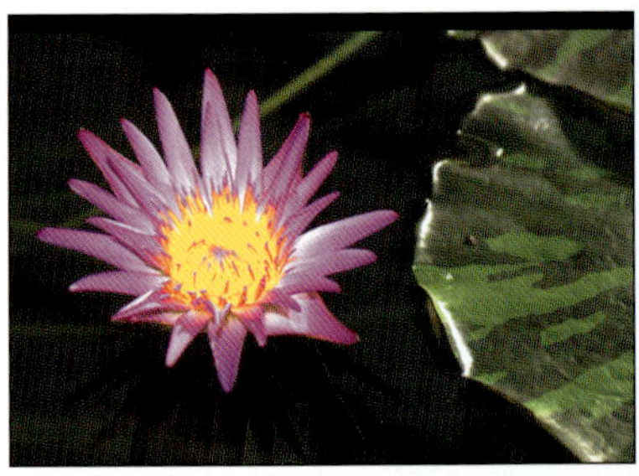

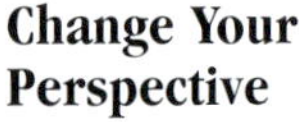

Change Your Perspective

If you don't have a zoom lens, step closer to your subject, but understand that it will change the perspective as well.

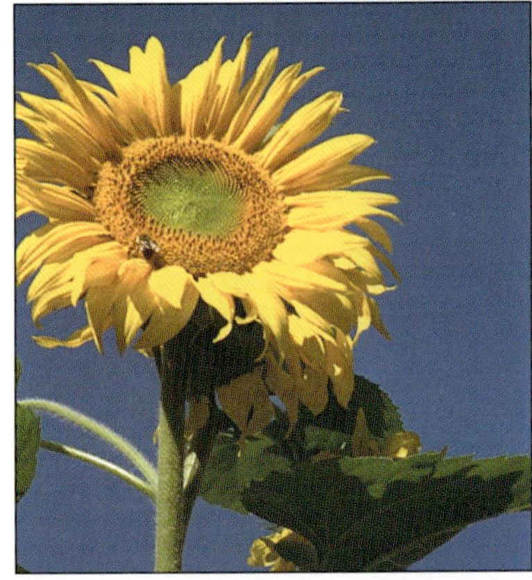

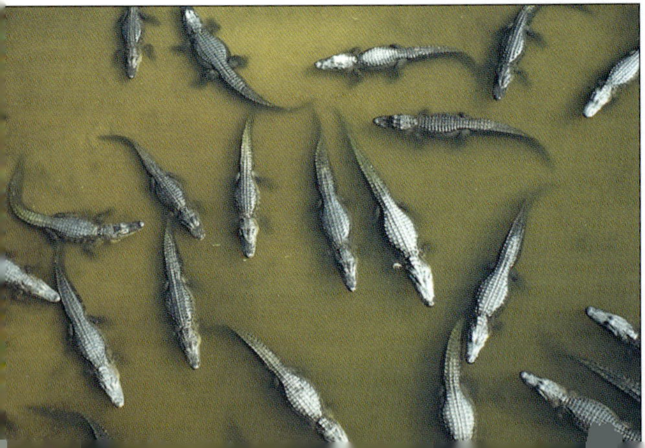

Shooting Angle

One of the rules stressed in this book was to shoot eye-level photographs of people. But you can have fun by sitting on the ground to shoot a wild portrait of your friend towering over you. Remember to turn the camera and take the picture as a vertical.

Similarly a photograph of a sunflower taken with the camera on the ground, pointed upward at the sky, can yield a dynamic picture. Likewise, you can choose a bird's-eye view (looking straight down) to shoot a bear track!

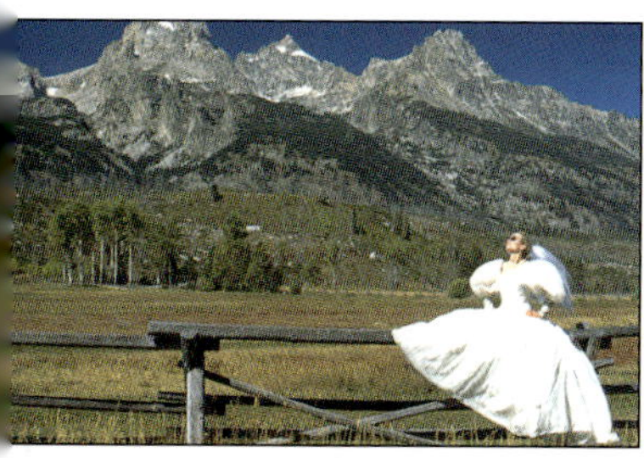

Background

With the exception of the type of photograph mentioned above, with a spectacular background, you'll generally want to strive for simplicity. Adjust your shooting angle until you can eliminate unwanted bold elements in the background, such as bright colors, written words (billboards or store signs), vertical lines (like telephone poles), horizontal lines, sunlit highlights, and shiny metal.

Foreground

If you study famous landscape photographs, you'll notice that many of them have "layers"

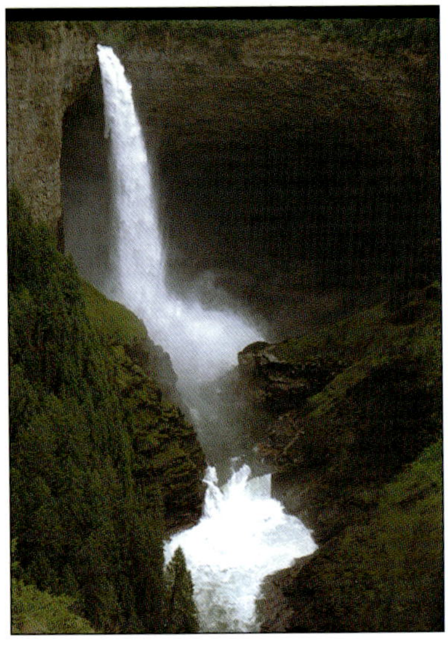

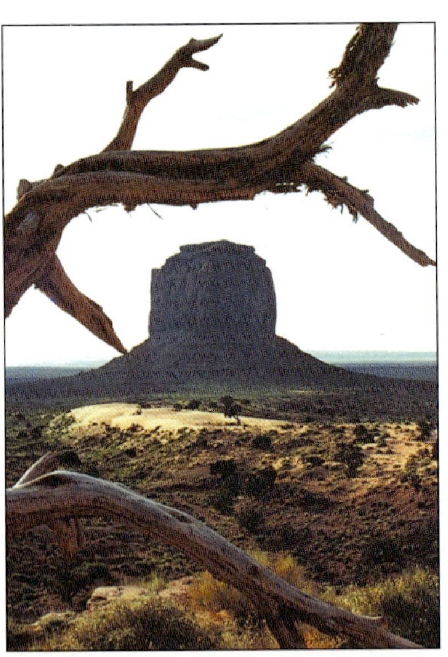

in the form of something in the foreground that is eye-catching; something interesting in the background; and sometimes something in the middle. For example, an interesting foreground element, like a rock or batch of flowers, draws your attention and provides scale for a majestic background, such as a mountain range.

Framing

In the same way that a pretty frame can accent and draw attention to a painting hanging on the wall, you can frame the subject of your photograph using objects found in the scene. Foreground elements, such as tree branches, doorways, or arches, can be used to focus the viewer's attention on the *real* subject, which is found in the midground or background of the photo.

The framing elements can be in focus

or out-of-focus, colorful or stark, elaborate or simple. Be careful, however, to make sure your camera's autofocusing system is locking in on the distant subject, and not accidentally focusing in on the framing elements. It is better to turn the flash off in these situations, because it may bounce off the framing element and either fool the exposure system into thinking it lit the distant subject (resulting in an underexposed picture) or it will overexpose the framing element turning it into a distraction.

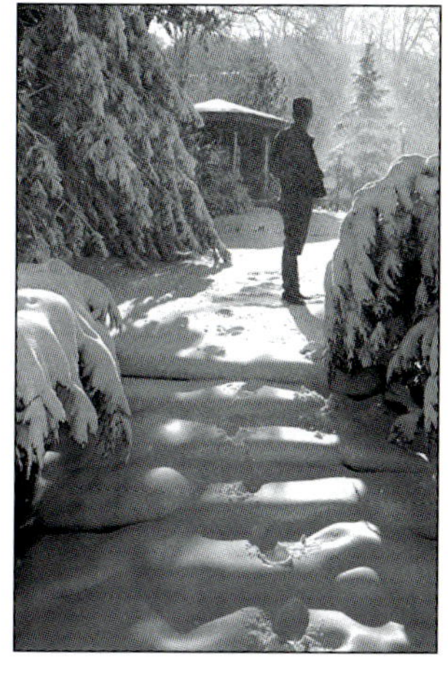

Pattern

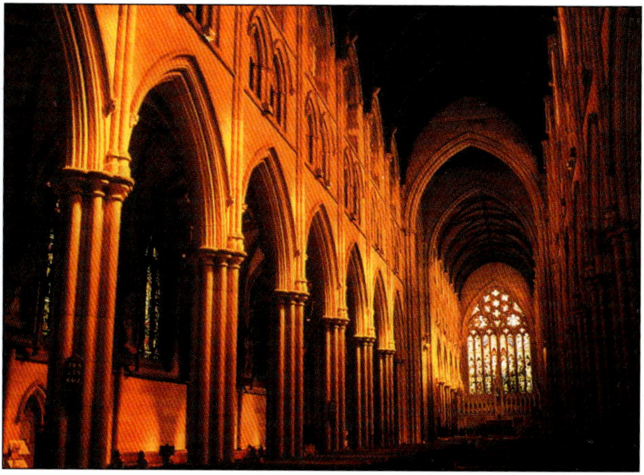

Patterns and repetition of form have been popular compositional elements among artists for centuries—and there is no reason why photographers shouldn't partake in the practice! The pattern can be created by light and shadow, such as the snowy path in the picture at right. Or it can be more literal; a repeating shape or object, such as a picket fence or a row of flower pots.

Take A Second Look

When you get that itch to take a picture, you've probably found a good subject. However, your first instinct on how to shoot it may not be the best, even if you're an experienced photographer. Take a moment to observe the scene in front of you, and think about the compositional hints presented in this book.

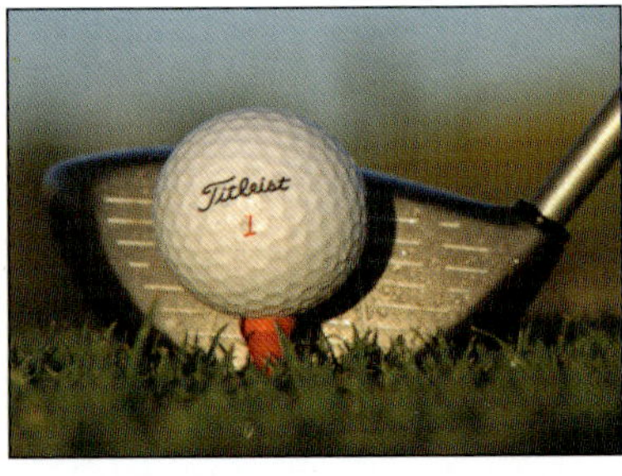

If you're worried about the subject "getting away," take that first quick shot, and then settle down for a carefully planned second shot.

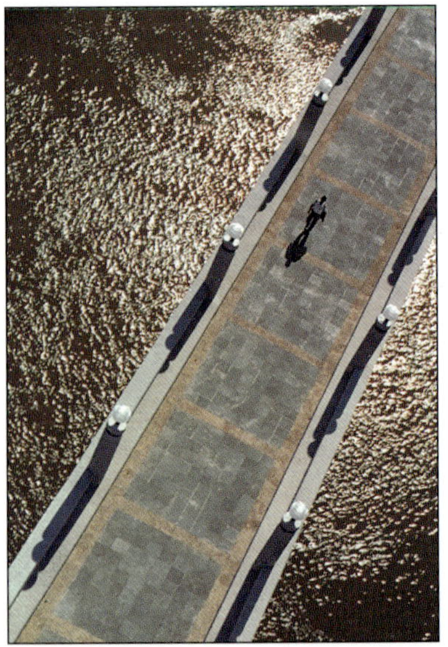

How Big Is It?

Anyone who has visited the Grand Canyon knows that photographs, even photos taken by professionals, just don't do it justice. That's because humans have wonderful depth perception that does not translate well to film. We can understand and feel the depth of the canyon. For this reason, when shooting broad landscapes or very large objects, you will want to include something in the photo that is a familiar size for scale or size comparison.

The same is true of small objects. A close-up photograph of a butterfly doesn't tell you if it is large or small. Snap a picture of it perched on a familiar flower and you instantly know if it has an enormous four-inch wingspan or if it is the size of your thumbnail.

Come Back Again

You can take this planning stage to extremes, and decide to come back for additional photos later or earlier in the day (for different angled sun), when the weather changes or even during a different season. Your results will change because the lighting, weather, and even your subject may change. We do this without realizing it, as we photograph our children growing up. (It's time-lapse photography in a sense.) You can also do this to document other important subjects, like your house and garden, your pets, the main street in town. You may be surprised at how different the same scene can look over days, months or years.

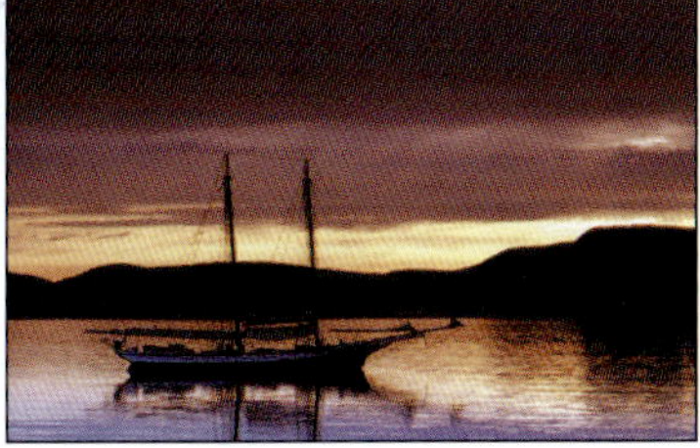

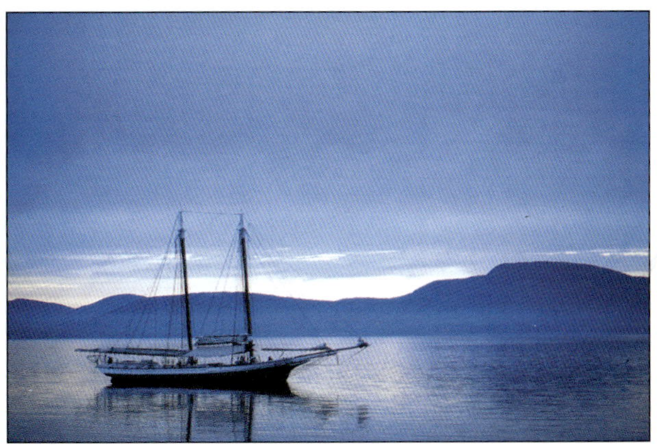

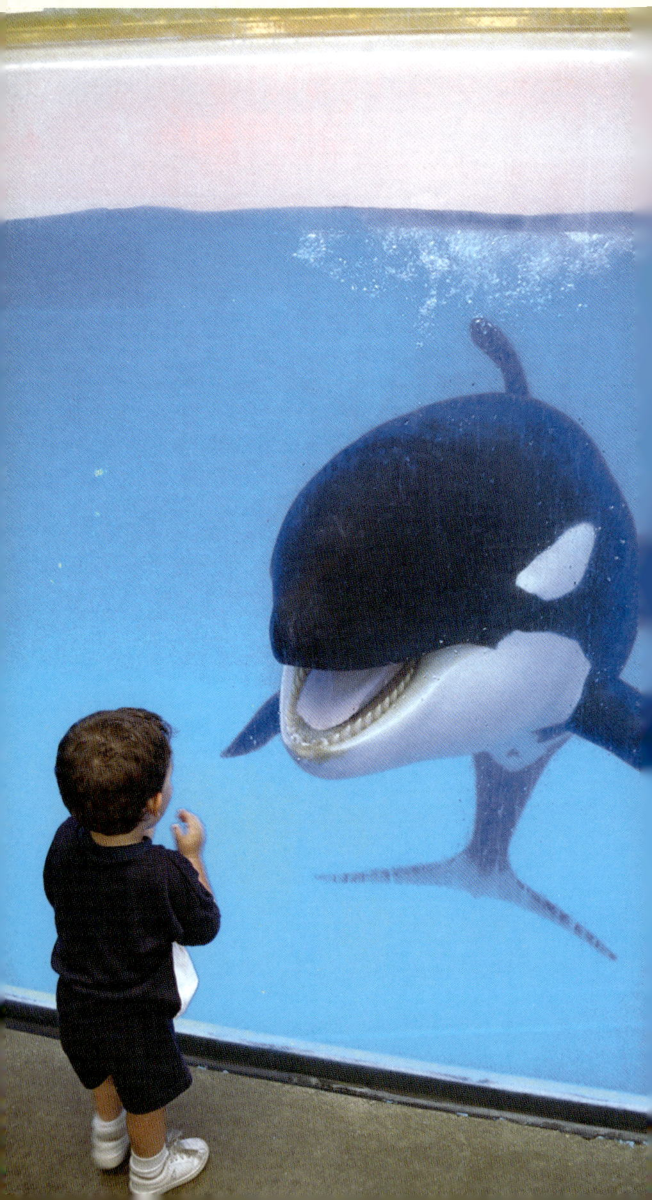

Travel and Vacation Photos

Vacations are some of the most memorable times of our lives. We abandon work to relax, travel, and have fun. Even work-related travel provides at least some opportunity to see new places and experience different cultures. Whether you're on vacation or working, there is no doubt that you'll want to save these experiences on film, to share with friends and to keep as a reminder of the trip.

What Should I Shoot?

Vacation and travel photographs can be divided into four basic types: the "I Was Here" pictures, the candid "Having Fun" snapshots, the "Slice of Life" images, and the classic, beautiful "Postcard" shots.

"I Was Here!"

My favorite type of travel photograph is what I call the "I Was Here" picture. You can buy a postcard of the Grand Canyon, but a picture of you and your family or travel companions in front of the Grand Canyon is a much more memorable souvenir. All too often, however,

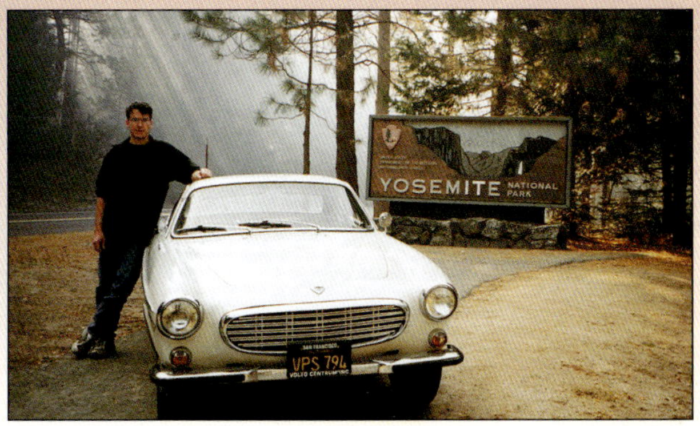

you come back from vacation and there are tons of shots of the family and companions and zero of the designated photographer. Even if you're camera-shy, years from now you'll regret it.

The easiest way to get this type of picture is to take turns shooting it. You're in the first picture, your traveling companion is in the second. Asking a fellow tourist or a passerby to take the picture is also a good method. Set your camera to auto and hope they do a good job framing the picture. If you bring along a small tripod, you can frame the shot exactly as you want it beforehand. This also allows you to set the camera's self-timer and jump into the picture if their are not any people around.

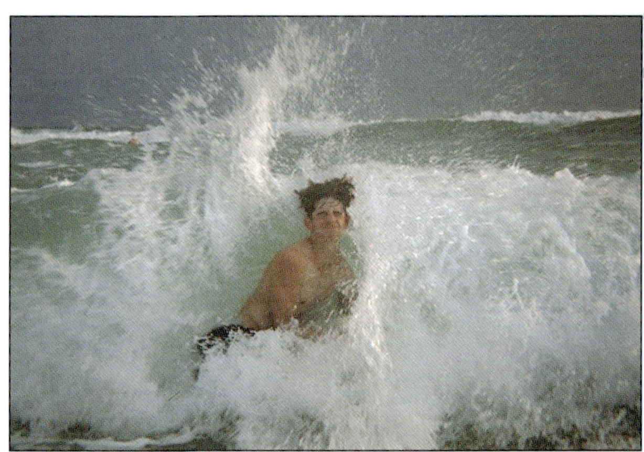

Take Candids, Too

Lining everybody up for a record shot at every scenic spot might get very old very fast, even with patient subjects. Take these photographs at key landmarks, and then spend the rest of the time taking candids of your travel companions. They will probably be so busy having fun and exploring the new territory that even the most camera-shy of them won't pay much attention to your picture-taking endeavors.

Slice of Life

One of the reasons we travel is to take a fresh look at life and experience different parts of the country and world. The more exotic your destination, the more different the culture and lifestyle of the area. Photographing the local folks involved in the rituals of daily life is a great way to remember the places you've visited and to share your experiences with friends and family when you return.

Get Perspective

Finding a high angle to shoot from can also give you a new perspective (literally!) on your destination. The eagle's-eye view is an especially wonderful vantage point for photographs. Look for observation towers, church steeples, bridges, and cliffs that you can access. Not only is it fun to watch the world from these observation points, but the pictures may be very memorable as well.

Don't go too high, especially if it's a cloudy or hazy day. The view from the Twin Towers in New York City is spectacular on a crystal clear day, but if there is haze in the air or low clouds, your view is greatly diminished. In fact, you may be better off in a 60-floor building from a photographic point of view.

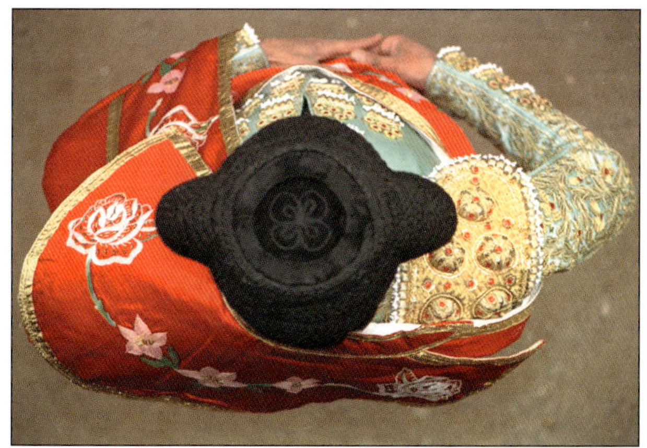

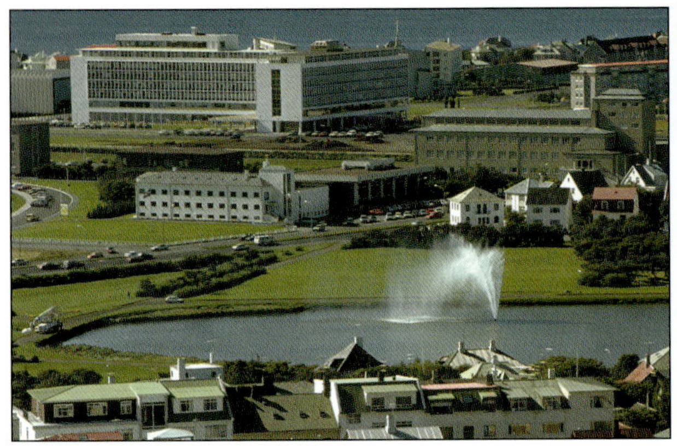

Scenic Flights

If you can afford a scenic air flight, I highly recommend it, especially when there are areas that would be difficult to access by land. A helicopter ride around the island of Kauai, Hawaii yields unbelievable photographs. It also takes you over areas that may be otherwise unaccessible.

If you're planning to shoot from a plane or helicopter, make certain you tell the tour operator first, so they can position you in the best seat for this purpose. Vibrations are a big problem, so do not try to brace your body against any part of the plane to steady yourself. This will only pass the vibrations into your body. Because the plane or helicopter is shaking and you're traveling at high speed, you'll need a fast ISO film to get sharp pictures. Select ISO 800 if it is available.

What Should You Bring?

First of all, are you happy with your camera? Do you like its size, handling, and performance. If the answer is no, the time to buy your new camera is before your big trip. Just give yourself enough time before your trip to practice with it. You don't want to be trying to learn the controls when that incredible photo opportunity presents itself! Even worse, you don't want to come home with nothing, because you did not understand one of the camera's basic functions.

Even with a tried-and-true camera, I can't stress enough the importance of testing your equipment when packing it for an important trip. If your camera is malfunctioning, you want to know this before you get to the bottom of the Grand Canyon. You don't want to discover the camera's battery is dead while you're out in the woods on a camping trip.

And remember to take plenty of film, extra batteries, and even a spare camera. A one-time-use camera makes a great backup

Processing on the Road

You don't have to wait until you get home to have your film processed. Take recommendations from the locals and go to a lab that offers fast turnaround. This, gives you the opportunity to reshoot a scene if the photo didn't come out like you expected. If you're visiting friends or relatives, you can present them with a small album or framed print to thank them for their hospitality.

Shooting Out of Windows

There are many instances when you want to shoot a scene through a window, but this presents some unique problems for point-and-shoot cameras, such as flare from flash or completely out-of-focus pictures.

Roll Down the Window

You can avoid most window problems if you can eliminate the glass by rolling it down. Obviously this is not an option on a commercial airliner!

Turn Off Your Flash!

If you can't roll down the window, turn off the flash. Otherwise you'll just get a photo of the flash re-flecting off the glass.

Use Infinity Lock

Your camera might try to focus on the glass, unless you tell it to focus on infinity instead. (Do this by using the Infinity Lock button, if your camera has one). Without Infinity Lock, you may end up with an out-of-focus picture of the window glass.

Clean the Glass

If possible, take a moment to clean the glass so spots and streaks don't show up in your photographs.

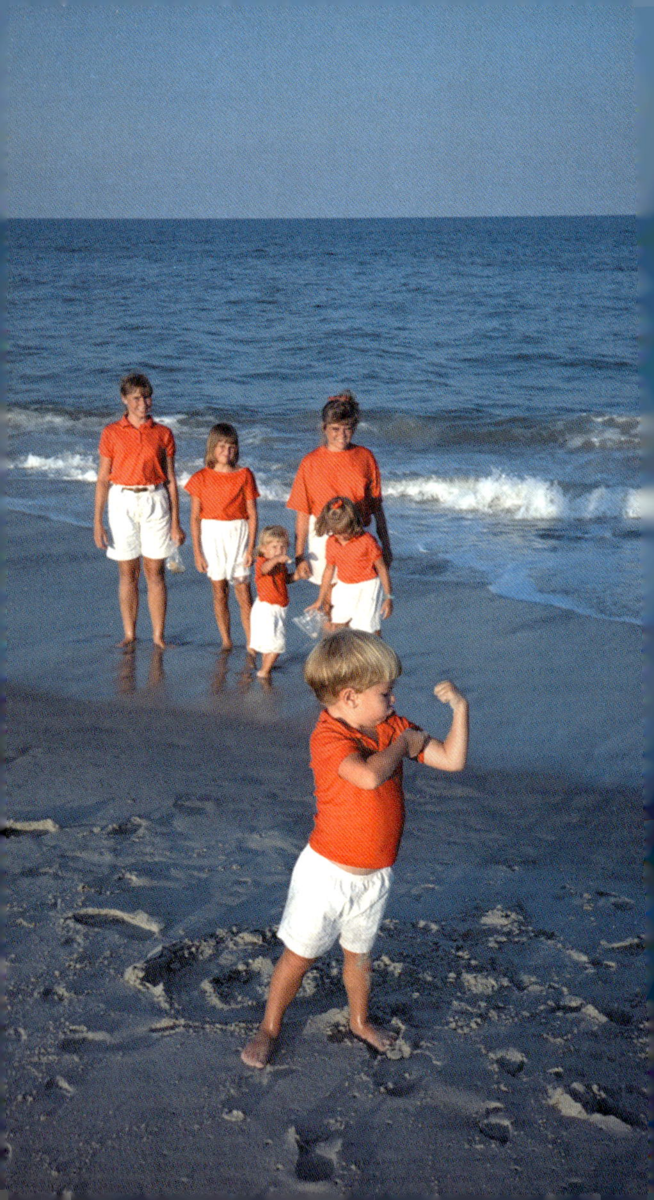

Family Albums

Once you've created pictures you're proud of, you then have the rewarding task of displaying and sharing them. There are whole new product lines of albums and frames available to fit prints of all sizes. Before you pick an album, determine if it is archival or photo-safe. Otherwise, your photos could fade in color and deteriorate.

To mail photos, you can purchase greeting cards with a cutout to hold a photograph or adhesive-backed postcards that stick on to your prints. You can also make your own cards by attaching photos to blank cards with photo corners or glue.

Sorting Your Photos

Even the best photographers in the world sometimes take bad pictures. It's perfectly okay to throw away the outtakes. In the photo business, eliminating less interesting shots is called "editing your pictures." It's a great practice for home users as well.

Unfortunately, the tendency is to say to yourself, "I paid for film and processing for these 24 prints, I'm going to keep every one." Resist this temptation. Why? For starters, you won't become overwhelmed with piles of pictures in a drawer or a shoebox in the back of the closet.

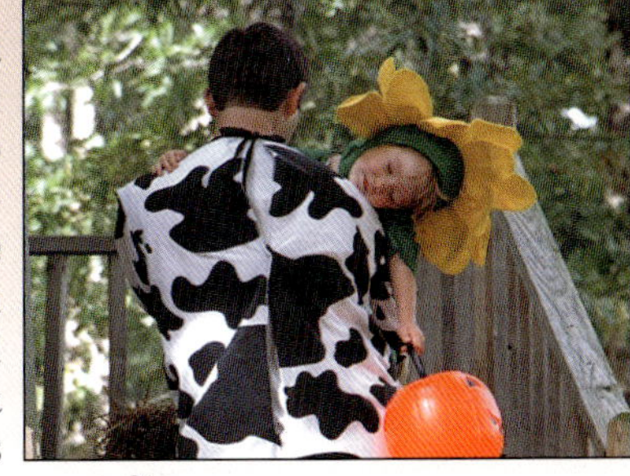

Even if you have a huge album to fill, you want every photo in it to be a unique, eye-catching shot. Two or three really great photos from Halloween can often tell the story better than a whole roll of film. This is

> **Toss It in the "Craft Basket"**
>
> Instead of ripping up the bad and mediocre shots, add them to your kids' craft basket. They'll have fun cutting and pasting the pictures to make collages and art projects.

because you dilute the impact of the good shots if you clutter up the album with lots of mediocre shots. For example, if you have a favorite photograph or two displayed in frames on your dresser, they have great visual impact and you notice them often. But if you were to then add 50 more to the dresser, that one great photo would be lost in the confusion and clutter. You probably wouldn't pay much attention to any of them, except when it's time to dust! And besides, on the rare occasion that you change your mind about a photograph you threw out, you can always reprint it from the negatives.

Having said this, I have to admit that editing your pictures is one of the most difficult photography tasks. Begin by discarding pictures that are technically or compositionally bad. Then, make two piles of prints—one in which your subject looks good, and one in which they don't. Toss the latter (and probably bigger) pile. Then get rid of the pictures that hold no particular importance to you–you know, the ones that make you ask "Why did I take this picture?" and "What is this a picture of?"

Part of learning how to become a better photographer is experimentation, but not every experiment is going to work. Just remember, the more you practice, the better your images will become.

Tell a Story

Aside from throwing out the bad shots, you'll want to think about the story you're trying to tell. An album is for sharing and remembering, so a picture or a series of pictures that tell a story are important.

Before you pick up your camera, and perhaps when you buy your film in preparation for the event, spend a few moments making a mental check list of possible shots. Just like a movie director, you need to ask yourself what "scenes" do I need to capture to tell the whole story of this event. You don't need to take all the shots you dream up, but it will prepare you should the opportunity arise.

For example, if your daughter is in her first dance recital, it's obvious you'll want to photograph the performance. But to tell the story of that recital, you may want to consider some of the following pictures as well:

- Your dancer practicing with the teacher the week before.
- Trying on her costume for the first time.
- Nervous backstage whispering.
- Dad helping her to lace her slippers before the performance.
- The highlights of the performance, of course.
- A picture of her brother in-tensely watching the show.
- A wide-angle shot of the stage with the audience applauding in the foreground.
- The celebration dinner afterwards.

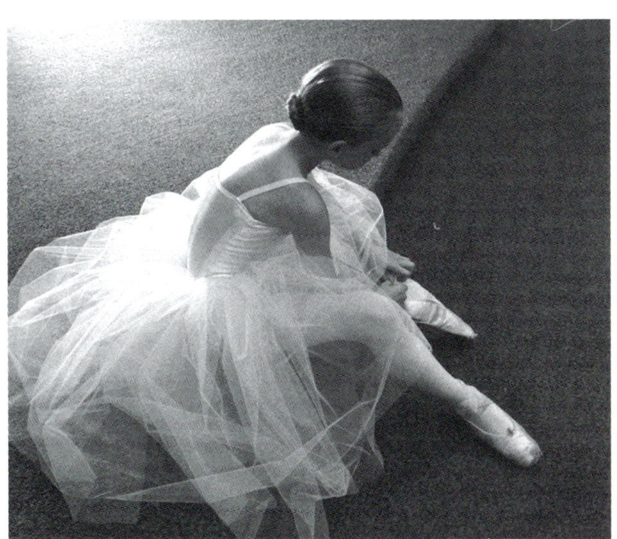

Sharing Your Album

When it comes to sharing your album with friends and family, you'll notice a big difference in the impact your album leaves if you've tried to tell mini-stories, and have edited out the lesser photographs. The viewers might not know why they're enjoying the viewing experience so much, but you will!

Choosing an Album

The album market has expanded enormously in the last few years, so that you literally have thousands of designs, sizes, and types to choose from. Most albums fall into one of the categories below.

Smelly Albums

Don't use them! If your album smells like plastic it is probably not archival and may cause gradual damage to your photographs. It will start by discoloring prints (often fading them to just reddish tones), and it might actually lift off the emulsion from the print. Put down this book and go sniff all your family albums. If any give off the tell-tale smell, I would seriously consider transferring the pictures to a modern archival album. Look for albums that are labeled archival, photo-safe, or acid-free.

"Magnetic Pages"

These albums were once very popular because they were so easy to use. Slip the photo under the clear plastic cover and it magically stuck in place. To bad these were some of the worst culprits when it came to destroying pictures. If you really love this style album, there are one or two manufacturers out there who make picture-safe versions.

Bound Slip-In Albums

These albums are great because it is easy to slip the photographs into clear plastic windows. Unfortunately, you are limited to the window sizes included. And if you want to intermix verticals and horizontals, your viewer is going to have to do a lot of turning the book this way and that. And you're completely out of luck if you frequently utilize the special panoramic and H-size print formats.

Binder Albums

Albums in binders take a big step toward correcting the format problems mentioned above, because you can mix the order of pages with different sized windows. Many people don't like the feel of a binder however, and prefer a bound album.

Scrapbooks

Unquestionably the most versatile type of album. If you enjoy craft projects, this is the album for you. You can secure photos (or other memorabilia) with archival glue sticks, two-sided photo tape, or photo corners. Add text, stickers, drawings, or dried flowers to make it a very personal and unique album.

The Most Modern Album!

Digital imaging has brought numerous innovations to the way we take pictures and also to the way we display them. The latest in frame technology is the "computer frame." The best way to describe it is an ultra-thin computer monitor inside a beautiful frame, which continuously displays your digital photographs in a non-stop slide show. These frames display images saved on storage media, such as the small memory cards used with digital cameras.

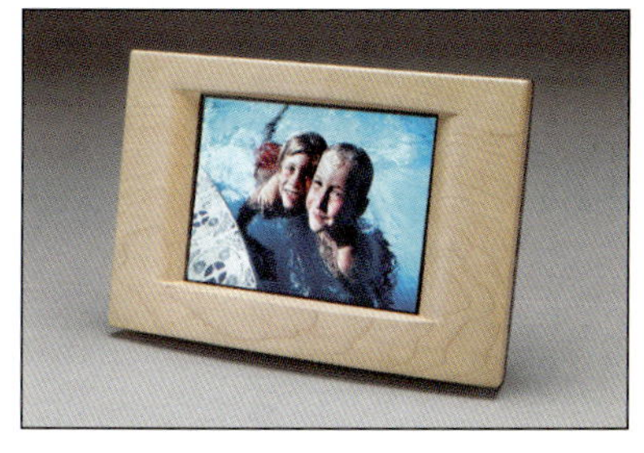

Archival Products

Whenever possible, buy albums, tapes, and glues that are labeled archival or photo safe, so they will not cause harm to your album. If possible, store your album in a cool, dry place. High humidity can cause the photos to stick to the pages or each other, and mold can grow. You put a lot of time into creating an album, and you want it to last.

Enlargements

After reading the tips in this book, your next photography session shoulkd produce some really terrific pictures—pictures so good, you will want to hang them on the wall!

Before having enlargements made, check the smaller prints carefully to make certain the picture is sharp. Any blurriness will be magnified in the enlargement. Most photofinishers can make standard-sized enlargements from your negatives to fit common frame sizes (5x7" and 8x10"). Proportionally, these standard sizes do not always match the ratio of the negative, so the image might need to be cropped. Ask the personnel at the lab to show you how much of the image you might "lose."

The KODAK Picture Maker can create custom enlargements and photo collages. Photos can be sized and cropped as desired. Text and borders can be added and simple retouching, such as removing red-eye, can also be done easily.

Matting and Framing

The most elegant way to frame a picture is to put it in a mat first. For example, you can purchase an 11x14-inch mat, with an 8x10-inch "window" cut out to display your picture. This mat fits into an 11 x 14-inch frame and the photograph is protected behind glass. The mat does two things: it is an elegant border between the print and the frame edge. Also it prevents contact between the print and glass, which can damage the print.

Precut mats are available at many photo stores in a variety of colors to complement your photo and your decor. Look for archival mats to help protect your pictures from fading and deterioration.

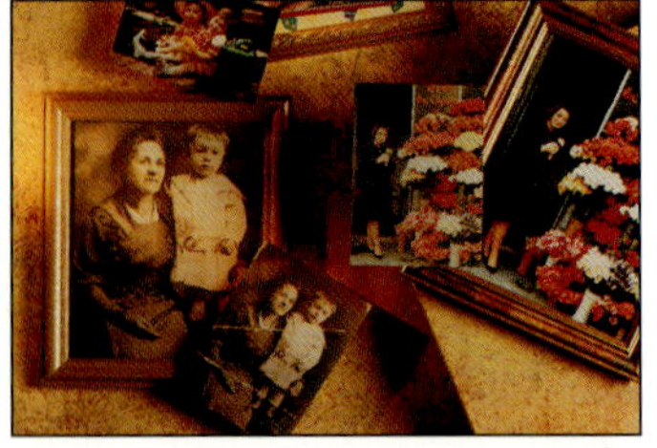

For special projects that require elaborate framing or unusual-sized mats, you can take your photos to a professional framer. Be sure to discuss the use of archival materials to preserve your images.

Good Intentions

Everybody always has great plans to photograph their family. What generally happens, however, is there is a plethora of photos when you first buy a camera, and then your output dwindles off to next to nothing in the following years. The best way to insure this doesn't happen is to make photography part of your lifestyle, and part of your family traditions. Always plan on bringing along your camera to family outings and sports events, and make holidays synonymous with picture taking. I like to keep my camera in a very accessible place, such as near where I hang my keys. That way, I remember to grab it as I'm rushing out the door.

Junior Photographers

Photography can be a fun hobby for kids. They've seen you take photographs for years, and often enjoy the chance to partake in documenting their family and friends. For toddlers, that means a toy camera. For five-year-olds and up it can be a one-time-use camera or child-oriented camera.

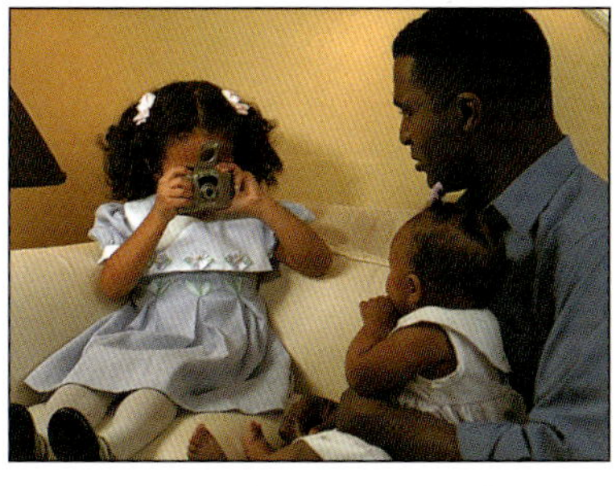

Depending on maturity, once your kids reach nine or ten years old, they're probably ready for an inexpensive point-and-shoot camera or digital camera. You can teach them the basics of camera care and shooting technique, and then give them a film and processing allowance along with plenty of encouragement.

Get them involved in the family album as well, helping to pick the shots that get included, drawing pictures for scrapbook pages, or deciding what pictures they would like enlarged and framed for their room. Getting to choose and maintain a small personal photo album can be a source of great pride for your kids.

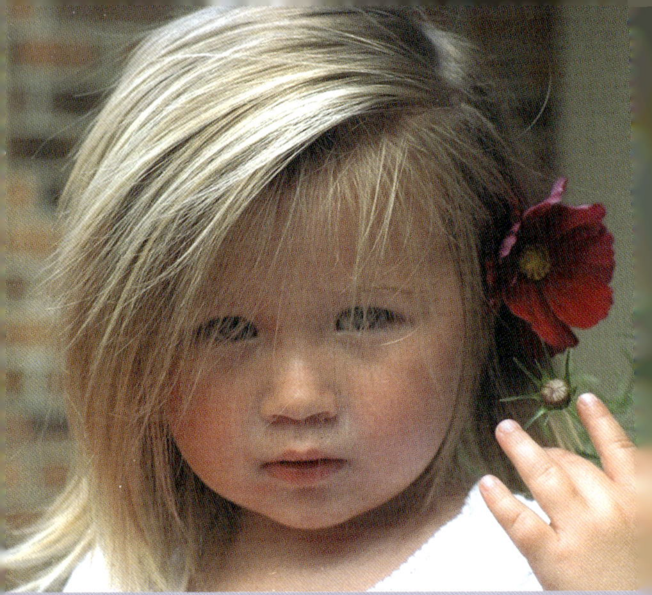

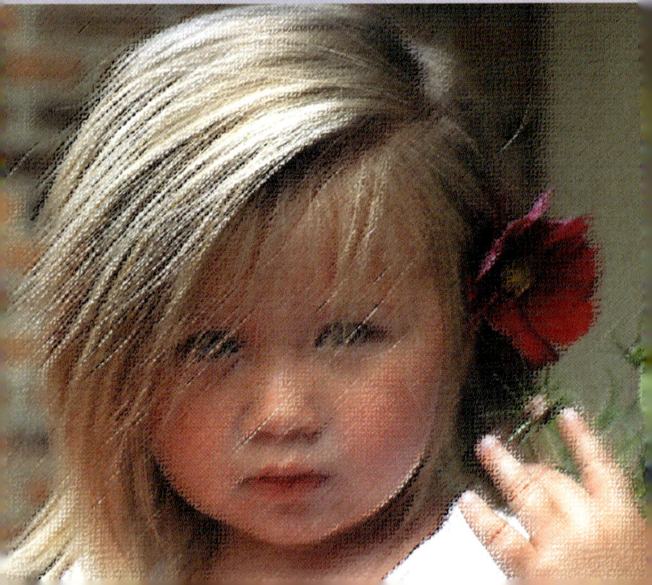

Photography and the Computer

Today it's easy for anyone with a reasonably modern computer to work with digital photographs. You don't need a digital camera, or any fancy equipment to get started. Armed with just a little bit of information, you can add photos to documents, send them in e-mail, and alter your photographs to achieve your creative desires!

What Is a Digital Picture?

A digital picture is simply a photograph that has been converted into "computer language" and saved as a file. Just like a word processing file, this picture file can be saved on your hard drive or a floppy disk, CD, or other media. It can be sent over the internet like e-mail or posted on a web site. To "read" this photographic file, you must have software that is compatible. Most picture software, for example, can show you what a common JPEG picture file looks like. Click on it, and the picture pops up on your computer monitor.

What Is a Pixel?

When an image is created either by a digital camera or a scanning device, it is recorded as many individual pieces, called pixels. Each pixel is assigned color and tonal values (limited only by the capability of the input device). The actual size of a digital image is usually stated in pixels–either the vertical and horizontal measurements, such as 300x450 pixels, or the total number of the pixels. In this example 135,000, since 300x450=135,000. This is called the pixel resolution, or resolution for short.

These pixels are evenly spaced. In the case of the 300x450-pixel image, they can be printed very closely together to create a small print that looks as smooth as a conventional photographic print. Or the image can be printed the size of a billboard, causing those 135,000 pixels to be spread out and enlarged into dots the size of golf balls.

Higher resolution picture files give you more choices, because you can print them at smaller sizes with good results, whereas you can't print low-resolution pictures big and hope to get photo quality. The downside is that a high resolution is larger, has longer processing times, and takes more computer memory space.

Digital Cameras

The quickest way to get your pictures into the computer, of course, is with a digital camera. But even if you own a digital camera, there are times you're going to want to reach back into your archives or family album and digitize your photographs.

Digital Photographs from Your Prints

Just because you're shooting your pictures with film, doesn't mean you can't do digital photography! There are a few easy ways to turn your prints, slides, and negatives into digital picture files.

Home Scanner

You can scan your prints, negatives, or slides at home with a scanner. Some are available for under $100, while professional models can cost well over $1000. It takes a little time to get the hang of scanning your images, but it soon becomes second nature.

Flatbed scanners are by far the most popular and easy to use. Like a photocopy machine, you simply lay your print or other flat art or fabric on the surface. They can be used in conjunction with optical character recognition (OCR) software to convert a printed page into a word processing file that can be edited on your computer! Some models offer accessory transparency adapters for film. Low-end scanners are good for small prints and e-mail pictures, but you usually have to spend quite a bit more for higher resolution models.

If you plan on doing quality (high-resolution) work with 35mm slides or negatives, you might need a film scanner. They are far more expensive on average than a flatbed scanner, but they are capable of enlarging the tiny film to large sizes. Though your flatbed might have a transparency adapter, it probably won't offer professional quality.

Home-use APS scanners are made specifically for APS film canisters.

If all you shoot is APS and you want to scan your film, it doesn't get easier than this. Simply insert your processed APS film canister and the scanner accesses the film, digitizes it, and displays a digital index print on your computer, with easy software interface.

Print- or sheet-fed scanners are usually very small, and very easy to use—but you can usually only scan prints up to 4x6 inches. The scanning resolution is also comparatively low.

Pictures on Disk

The easiest way to get your photographs "digitized" is to use a photofinisher that offers this as an option. For a few extra dollars, you'll receive prints as well as a disk or CD with digital files for every image on the roll.

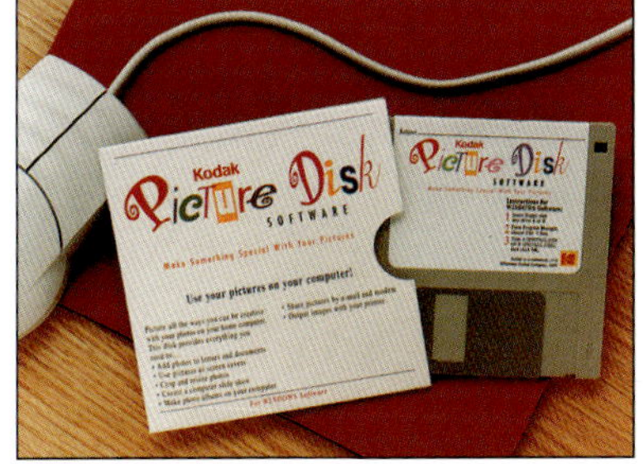

Free software supplied with the disk, CD, or on the Kodak web site will allow you to view your images; you'll be offered picture editing tools for automatically improving the color and contrast; and creative tools for "stylizing" the image. Software for e-mailing, printing, and organizing your pictures is also included.

KODAK PHOTONET OnLine

If you have internet access, a more convenient alternative to floppies or CDs is to have these images posted on the Kodak PhotoNet online. You are given a private password to access your pictures. Simple, interactive e-mail order forms let you purchase prints or photo novelties. For a small monthly membership, you can also use the network as your online photo library and permanently store your photos. You can share your password with friends and relatives, who can look up the pictures and order their own reprints directly. You no longer have to guess which pictures in what sizes they'll want to own. You can even delete the bad or embarrassing images before sharing your password.

Digital Pictures from Other Sources

Images can be received by transmission via e-mail attachments or modem lines. You can also have scans made at the same time you have your traditional film developed; these digital files can then be posted on the internet where you (and friends and family) can use a password to view, download, e-mail, or print.

The latest moving image recorders are digital video (DV) camcorders or DV. DV records hours of motion and sound. Most provide a simple way to save still images from motion clips.

Clip art and other copyright-free photographs are available from many software companies as well as government organizations. They are available on floppy disk or CD, or you can download them off the internet. Then combine them with your own photographs to create original art.

Picture File Formats

If you've spent a lot of time on the computer, you probably know that there is a wide range of software available. Many of these packages use proprietary file types. You can't always take a spreadsheet file and drop it in a word processing program unless they are compatible. The same is true for picture files. Your digital pictures must be saved in a file format that can be recognized by the software of your choice.

File formats go in and out of vogue as technology and consumer

Copyright Warnings

Just because you are able to scan it, doesn't mean you can legally use it! Most photos and artwork printed in magazines, books, brochures, or the newspaper are covered by the same copyright laws. "Borrowing" the image is like "borrowing" items off the shelf of a store.

You can use most images for your personal enjoyment, but as soon as you start displaying, distributing, or trying to sell them, you'll be infringing on the rights of the artists, photographers, and models. This includes portrait and wedding photography!

preferences change. But there are several you will probably run across a lot. Certain file formats are platform-independent, meaning they can be opened easily with a PC or a Macintosh computer. Others are linked to specific photo software. Some offer compression options to shrink their file size temporarily (albeit at the cost of some quality).

JPEG (.jpg) is a compression file format that can produces a small file size with minimal loss of detail. For some professional uses anything that reduces image quality is unacceptable, but for home use, JPEG is very useful. JPEG is a good file format for photos, but are generally not a good choice for text, line art, signatures, and sharp-edged graphics.

The KODAK PHOTO CD Image Pac file format and FLASHPIX file formats are very effective. Both are multi-resolution formats, offering the same image in either five or six file sizes in each Image Pac file. This means you can choose the resolution that works best for your immediate application—such as low resolution for internet enjoyment, and high resolution for large prints.

The TIFF format is another very popular professional format for photographs. It is used extensively in desktop publishing, but is usually a relatively large file size.

Once in the Computer

Once you have a digital picture file, you can bring it into your computer. At this point, the options are endless. You can alter the picture, combine it with other photos or text, and then utilize it in documents, output it onto paper, or create outrageous photo crafts.

Changing the Picture

There are many professional home picture editing and manipulation programs. Some allow you to change the picture pixel by pixel, while others make quick and easy alterations in one sweep. Image alteration techniques fall into two broad categories:

- Photographic effects: Contrast control, color and tonal enhancements, cropping, rotating, retouching, blur, multiple exposures, etc.
- Artistic enhancements: Painting styles, tracing, texturizing, smudging, collaging, tracing, stretching, "goo-ing," morphing and many other fun options

Computer Fun

Once you've altered or corrected your images, there are hundreds, if not thousands, of things you can do with them. For starters, you can include them in documents, such as memos, reports, presentations and school homework assignments.

Service providers can make huge prints for your wall from your digital photographs. You can also have your images printed on watercolor paper, special papers and canvas.

Ever consider using photographs and personalized type on your gift wrap paper? You can design it yourself or use easy software to make custom gift wrapping paper with your ink-jet printer. You're only limited by the size of the paper your printer can handle.

Greeting cards and postcards have never been easier than today. Kodak and other manufacturers make prescored or die-cut papers and software templates just waiting for your images and type. Alternately, your can get multiple prints from the photo lab and slip them into "paper frame" cards, or adhere pre-printed postcards on the back.

Your family can publish its own newsletter. It's a great way to keep friends and relatives up to date in less time than it takes to write a stack of individual letters.

Photo mugs, mousepads, jigsaw puzzles, and even cookies and cakes are just a few of the photo novelties available. Some are do-it-yourself kits for your home printer, while others require that you send your prints or transmit your digital files, then wait for the product to be delivered.

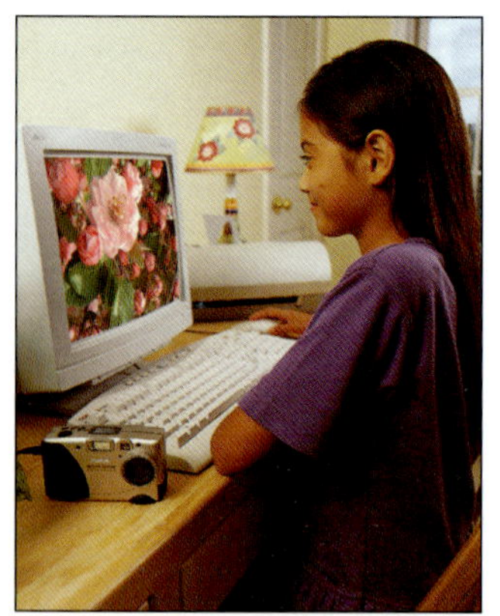

Service providers can turn your photos into actual oil paintings with a machine that has a computer-guided reproduction system. It uses digital photo files to create a plotting

Digital Fun With Your Photos

There are hundreds if not thousands of computer programs that let you be creative with your digital photographs. You can get a taste of these fun experiments by visiting the KODAK PICTURE PLAYGROUND at www.kodak.com. You can create wonderful variations of your photographs with a click of the mouse.

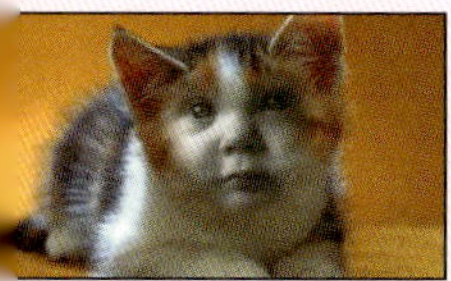
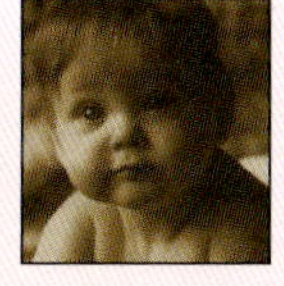
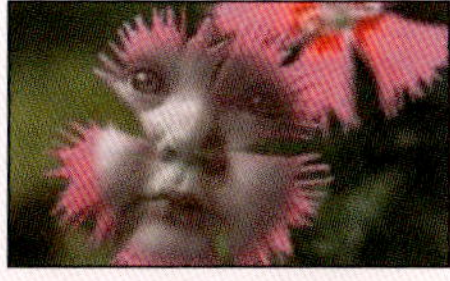
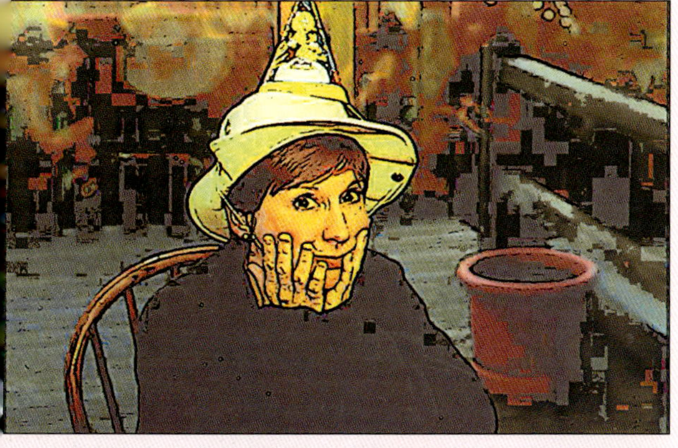
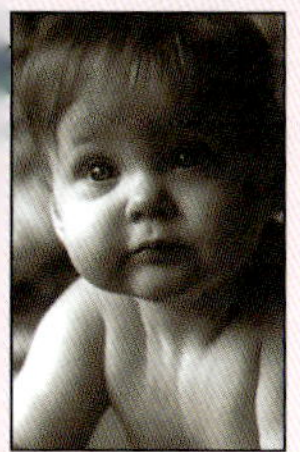
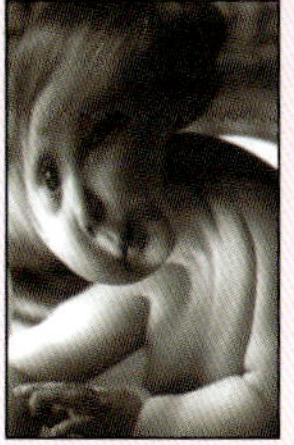
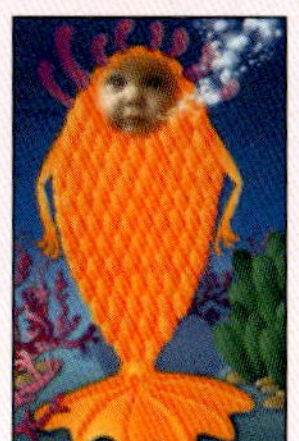
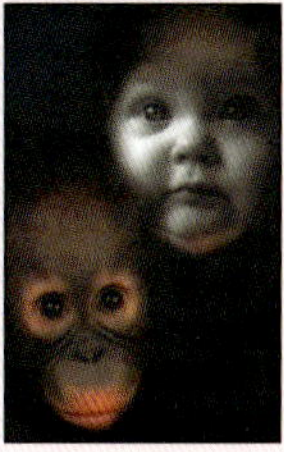

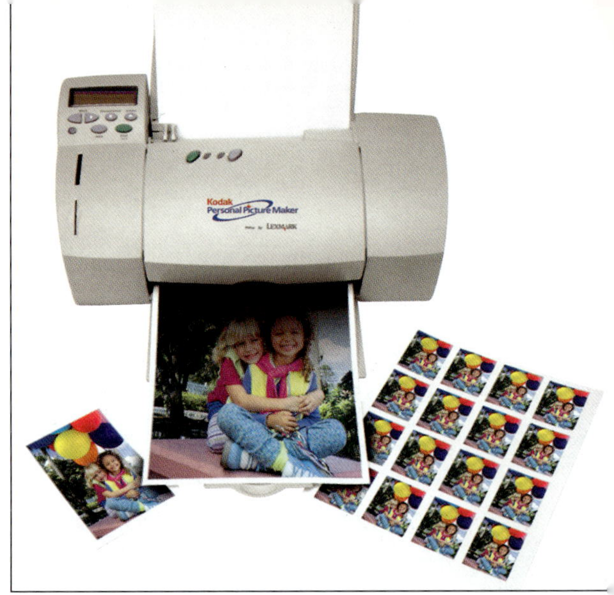

device, which in turn lays down oil paints to produce a painting. Custom color palettes are available.

Self-adhesive stickers are terrific for family projects or bumper stickers made to order on your own computer. Self-adhesive polyester sticker papers can be run through many home and office printers. They come in novelty sizes and colors, or the standard office selection from file folder labels to address labels to full sheets. With laser printers, be sure to use the special heat-resistant variety.

You can run special iron-on transfer paper through your ink-jet, thermal wax, or dye sublimation printer to create images that can be transferred to cloth fabric with an iron. Great for T-shirts, quilts, or custom garments.

On your computer, photos can be used as screensavers and desktop backgrounds.

Certificates and awards are now available with embossed or colorful edges and a blank center for adding a photo and text.

Terrific software packages create digital photo albums. You can elect backgrounds, mats, photo sizes, and page layouts. Then you can add headlines, captions, or funny cartoon bubbles. Best yet, it's easy to print multiple copies for relatives and friends, or distribute them on the internet.

Sophisticated collaging software, and collaging functions within other photo software, allow incredible control and creativity.

Quilters will be thrilled to learn that you can add photos to quilting patches! Either use specially made patches for the ink-jet printer, or use T-shirt transfer materials and iron it on to your favorite fabrics.

Fantasy magazine covers are always a favorite with kids. They can be the star of a sports magazine cover, or make a Mother of the Year cover as a birthday gift.

You can even create personalized coloring books and comic books for children, based on their own photos with easy to use templates and software designed for the purpose.

Genealogy and family tree programs are enormously popular and easy to create. They coach you through the process. Most help you create a visual family tree with photos as well as memorabilia. Others give you hints and suggestions for writing diary or autobiographical pages. The best kits include questionnaires for your family members; get contributions from distant as well as close relatives.

Digital time capsules are great fun and easy to create. Use special

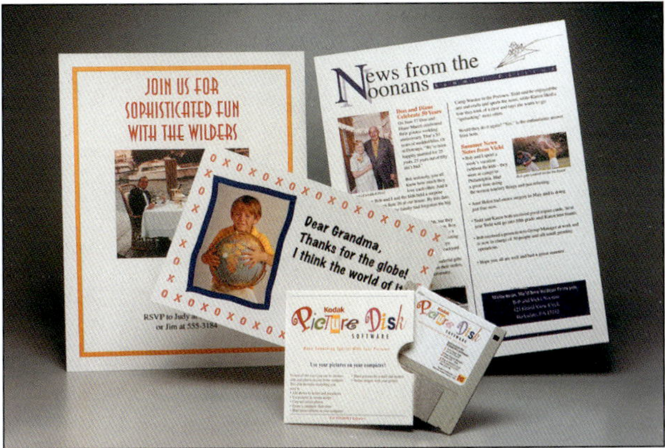

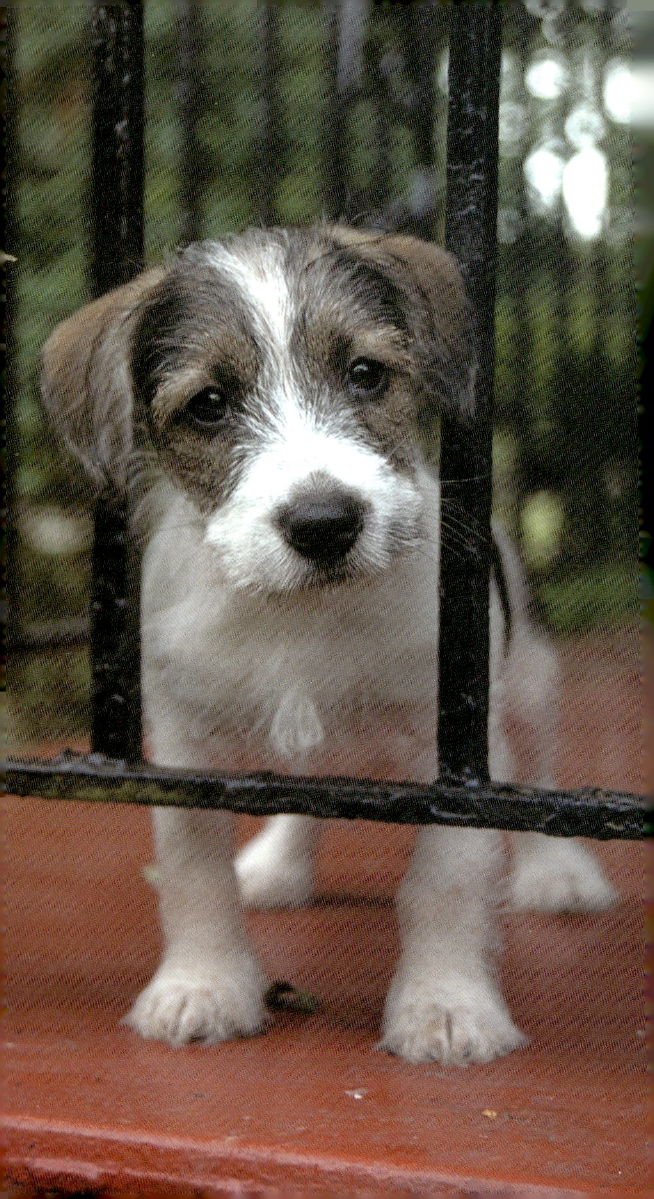

Printing Your Digital Photos

Outputting your pictures can range from "soft viewing" (looking at them on the computer monitor) to photo-quality printing on your ink-jet printer.

Starting Out

Most computer monitors give a luminous phosphor display, capable of millions of colors. Yet while your photograph looks fantastic on the monitor, you may be in for a surprise when you send it to the printer. The mere fact that monitors are based on emitted light, and the prints are seen with reflected light, insures that the images can never be quite the same. Monitor viewing also does not require high-resolution images. The output capability or resolution of most monitors is about 72 ppi (pixels-per-inch). Thus if you want an image to appear as a 4x6-inch snapshot on the monitor screen, you only need a low resolution of approximately 300x450. This same resolution image would look very poor printed out on an ink-jet at 4x6 inches.

Ink-Jet Printers

Ink-jet printers are by far the most popular home printers. You may encounter other types of printers (laser, thermal wax, dye-sub and more) in the office and professional setting, but these are outside the scope of this book. In general, ink-jets offer very smooth gradations of color. Special "photo" papers and inks further improve the photographic quality. Many printers can take specialized papers and substrates. On the downside, they are extremely slow and are susceptible to smudging, the paper

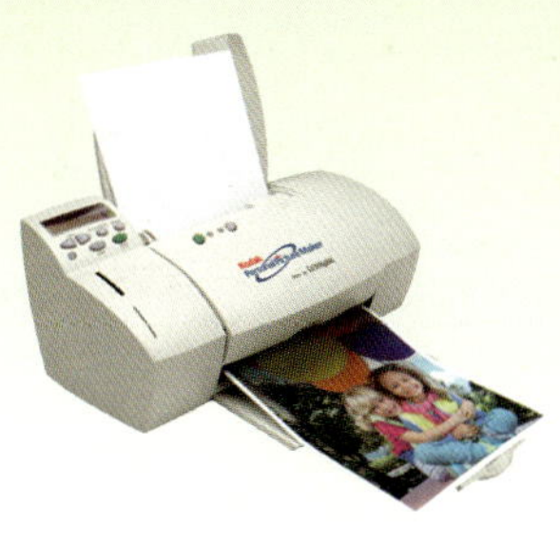

and inks can be expensive. Also, unless you use the new archival inks, they quickly fade in normal display conditions.

Archival Inks

You might love your ink-jet results, but unless you're using the new archival inks or a special UV coating, they are going to fade in a matter of weeks, if not sooner. You are better off going to a service provider for your enlargements, making certain you ask specifically about long-term archival qualities. As you might expect, silver halide-based digital prints are much more permanent.

Sending Images

One of the joys of digital photography is being able to share images quickly with friends, family, clients, vendors, and others. Of course, this can be done by handing a removable storage disk (like a floppy, CD or Zip) to a friend. But the faster, more convenient method is to transmit the

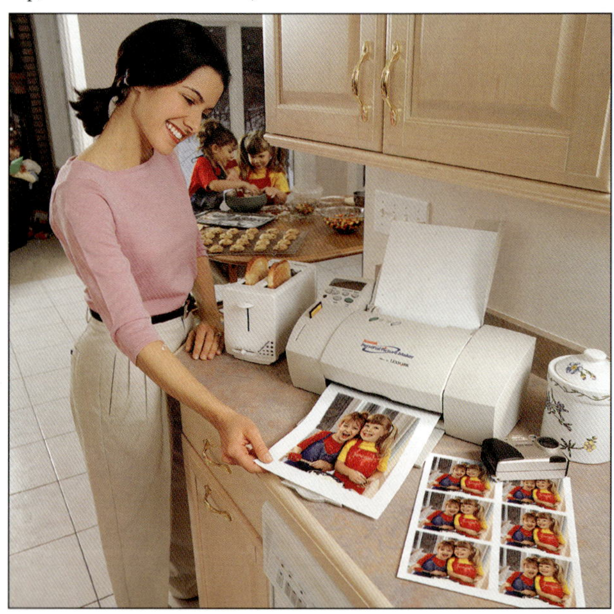

information from one computer to another via modem or the internet.

Modems allow your computer to "talk" to another computer over ordinary telephone lines. They can be used to access the internet. Modems are inexpensive, small, and portable, and can be used almost anywhere you find a telephone line. However, they are very slow to transmit large files compared to cable modems and digital lines. A big problem with modems is that one small glitch on the phone line could bring the process of uploading (sending data) or downloading (receiving data) to a full stop.

Cable modems offer exponentionally faster hook-ups to the internet, as do digital signal lines—but these services are not available everywhere, and usually come at a premium price.

The Internet

The internet is great for recreation, communication, research, and shopping. Internet service providers, like AOL or your local cable company give you a gateway to the internet. You log on to the internet through this company, via phone modem, cable modem or other means. Most larger internet service providers bring you onto their home page, where you will find member services, like a mail center for sending and receiving e-mails, access to chat groups, customer service, online technical support, games, prizes, and more. You can use the home page as a starting point for accessing the rest of the internet.

E-mail

Probably the most often used function of the internet is e-mail. Letters, data, spreadsheets, and documents of all types can be attached to e-mail, in addition to photographs. It's faster than mail or overnight couriers, and it's a lot cheaper. Plus, you can indicate multiple recipients to send one e-mail to dozens of people simultaneously.

If you decide to attach pictures to e-mail, you'll need to think ahead as to how the photos will be used. If your recipient is only interested in soft viewing, then attach a low-resolution version of the picture. This will keep the frustration level low when the recipient is accessing the picture, since downloading times for higher-resolution images can take minutes or even hours with a slow modem.

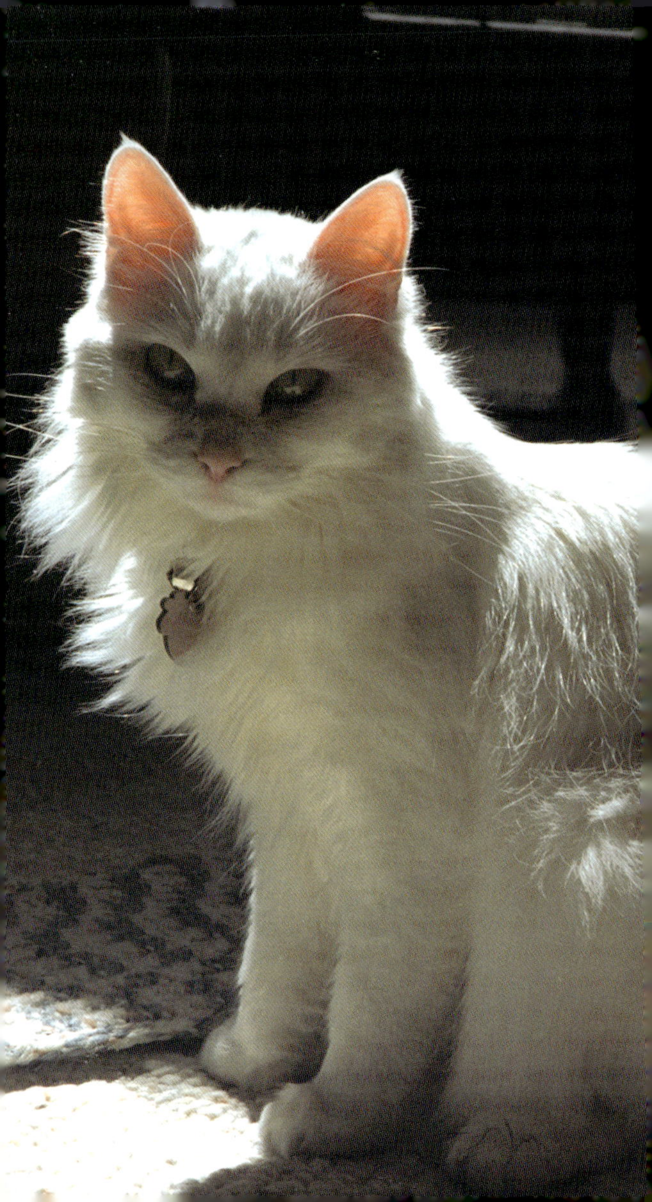

Troubleshooting

It can be very frustrating to eagerly await the return of your photos from the photo lab, only to be disappointed when you get the results. Sometimes it may be an error on your part, but it could also be poor processing or an equipment malfunction. The following sections will help you get started in troubleshooting your own pictures.

Blurred Pictures

Blur is sometimes mistaken for poor focus, but they actually look different and are caused by different problems.

Whole Picture Is Blurry

This is caused by camera shake. In low-light conditions or with slow speed films, the camera sometimes has to use long exposures to make the picture. You can tell it's a long exposure, because instead of going "cli-click", there is a pause between the clicks. You can fix this three ways: Brace the camera on a solid object or steady it with a tripod; switch to a higher speed film; or use a flash.

Subject Is Blurry

When the camera has to use a slow shutter speed (such as in low light conditions or with slow speed films), an action subject can move during the exposure, and this movement is captured on film as a blur. You can avoid this by switching to a higher speed film, or using flash if the subject is close.

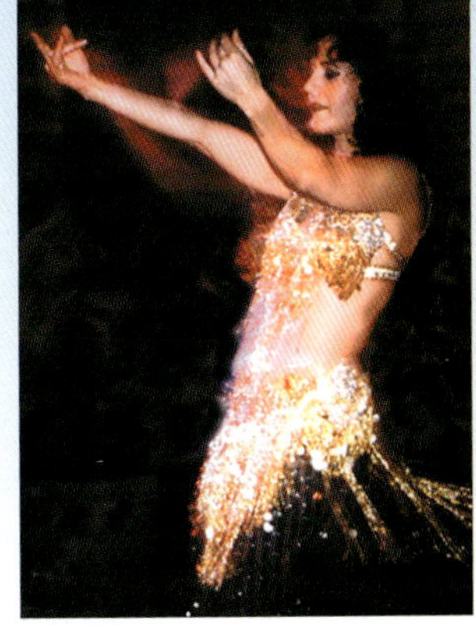

Is It Blurred or Out-of-Focus?

It is important to know the difference, because the problems of blur and incorrect focus are caused by very different things.

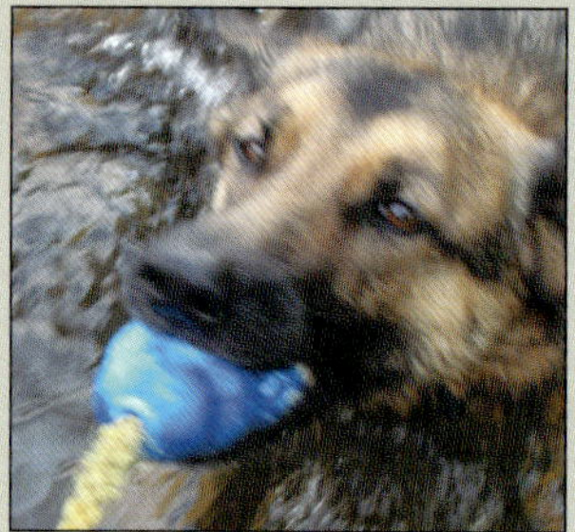

Blur from Camera Shake

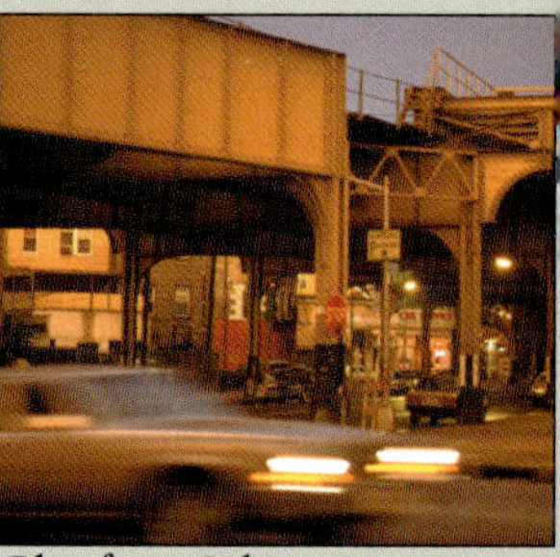

Blur from Subject Movement

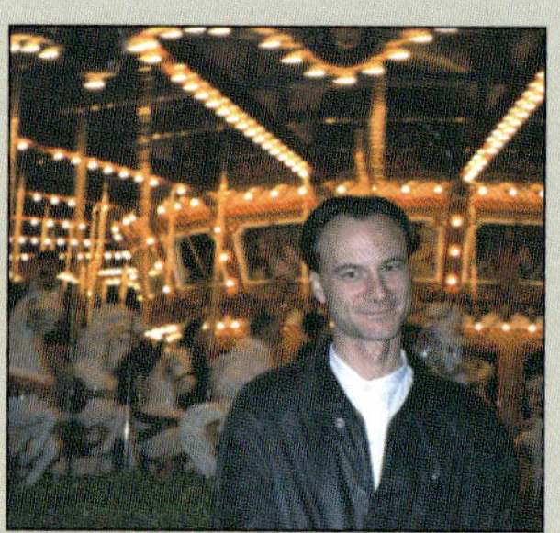

Background Moved

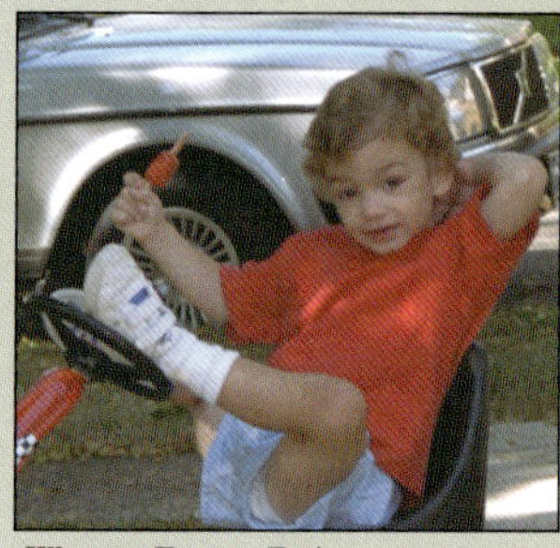

Wrong Focus Point

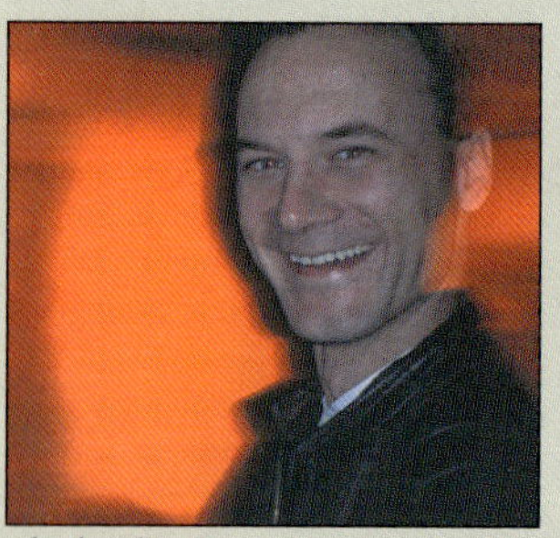

Flash Ghosting

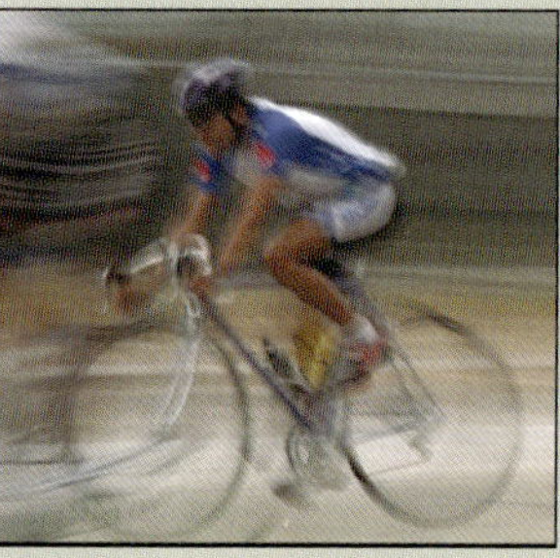

Panning

Background Is Blurry

You and the subject are not moving in comparison to each other, but the background is moving in comparison to the camera. And example is taking a picture of a friend in front of a ferris wheel. The friend is standing still (so he records sharp on film), but the moving amusement park ride records as a blur.

Panning Blur

If you're shooting action in low light or with slow film without flash, you can "pan" with your subject (follow them in the viewfinder) during a long exposure. This causes your subject to remain relatively sharp, while the background blurs. This is a very popular special effect technique with professional photographers.

Whole Picture Is Out-of-Focus

Either you are too close to your subject (beyond the focusing capability of the camera), or the camera was unable to achieve focus. One common problem is shooting through windows, because camera tries to focus on the window, instead of the scene outside. In these cases, a camera with an infinity lock function is helpful.

Part of Picture Is Out-of-Focus

There are two possiblities, misfocused or you don't have enough depth-of-field. The former problem can be overcome by using the focus-lock function on your camera. Most point and shoot cameras are heavily center-focus oriented. If you subject is even a little off center, you may need to center the camera on the subject, press the shutter button half way down, and then recompose while holding the button down.

The second problem occurs when using slow speed films, shooting in low light, focusing close to your subject or using "portraiture" mode. All three of these factors can cause the camera to take pictures with "limited depth of field", in which not everything from foreground to background is in focus. It can be countered by adding flash, using faster film, stepping further away or switching to "landscape" mode.

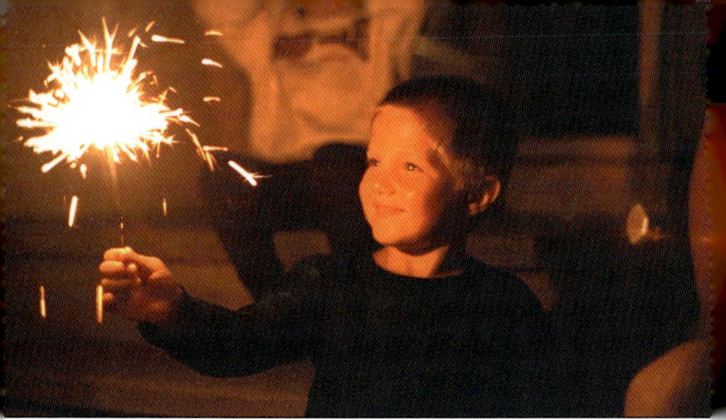

Color Casts

The most common reason your photos might have a color cast is the lighting. Most films are made to be used in daylight or with flash. If you use fluorescent or incandescent light, the photo may have an unnatural or unpleasant color balance overall.

Heat damage to film often shows up as an uncorrectable green or pink cast. Be careful not to let your camera or film get hot; never leave it in the hot car or near a sunny window.

Color casts are most easily seen in the light areas of the photograph, so caucasian fleshtones are greatly affected, and snow scenes can be problematic.

Another common problem is pink skin. The "opposite" color of green is pink. If a photofinisher tries to make a picture less green, they can overdo it and turn it too pink.

Use a quality photofinishing service that stands behind their work. If your prints have a color cast, ask them to reprint your order. They may be able to adjust the color to look more natural when they make your prints.

Digital Solutions

Damaged Prints

If this same print is damaged from age or rough handling it can be digitally fixed as well. Amazing new technology in some scanners will automatically correct and repair scratches and dust. Simple software programs can automatically recolor faded pictures or retouch creased pictures. When the utmost quality is needed, the digital picture file can be manually retouched by an expert (although it can get expensive).

Digital Retouching

Images can also be retouched digitally. In fact the conventional methods of retouching prints and negatives is a dying art form. Digital retouching can be as simple as removing red-eye from a portrait or as complex as compositing many scenes together. It's great fun to play with photo-editing software to enhance photographs through retouching.

Images can be retouched to correct or improve colors. Early morning shadows can cause some pictures to look excessively blue. You can remove unwanted elements from a composition, for example, a telephone pole can be very distracting if it "spouts" from behind your subject's head. All of these things can be "cured" in photo editing software programs.

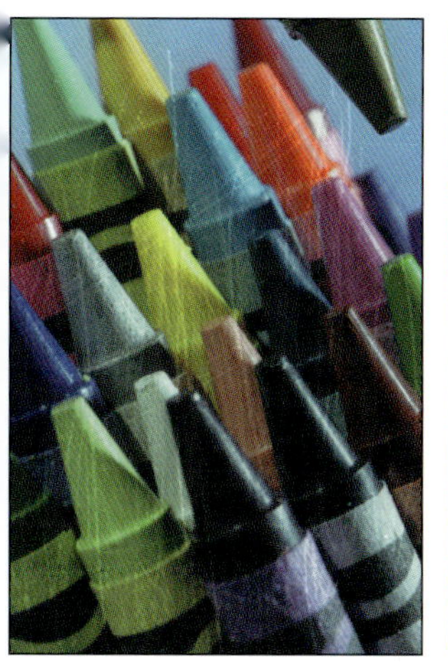

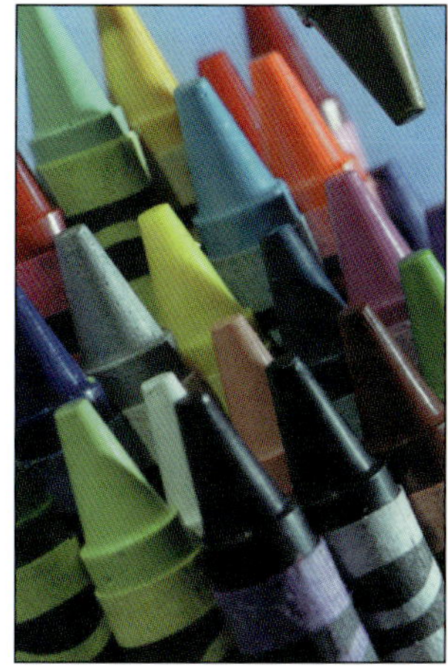

With the proper software, digital retouching can salvage even badly scratched negatives.

Lost Negatives

The new digital world has made lost negatives no big deal—as long as you still have a print. You can scan the print at home or have your photofinisher do it for you. This creates a digital version of the print that can easily be printed.

Dark Prints

These are some common causes of dark prints:

• If your subject is very light, such as a snow scene, it can be difficult for even a sophisticated camera to expose it correctly. Fortunately, most print films can produce acceptable images even if the exposure wasn't perfect. Ask your photofinisher to try making a lighter print.

• The subject is beyond the flash range. You are trying to light up a subject who is beyond the reach of your flash. Most point-and-shoot cameras can't light up a subject more than 20 feet away with ISO 200 film.

• You are using auto flash indoors with slow-speed film. Your subject may look perfectly fine, but the more distant background will be dark. Switch to faster film and keep the flash on, turn on lights in the room, or both.

• The photofinishing lab printed the images too dark.

Dull Prints

Prints are usually described as "dull" if they have low contrast. Possible causes of dull prints are:

• Overcast dull lighting produces dull prints. If your subject is nearby, try popping it with fill-flash to bring out the colors.

• Film damaged by heat can lose contrast and color saturation.

• Photos shot weeks or months before the film was developed can sometimes fade. Don't wait! Have your film processed shortly after the photos are taken.

• Poor processing of otherwise normal photos can cause dull prints.

Flare

Flare can sometimes be very obvious (a big bright spot or starburst of light in the picture). It can also reduce contrast and produce uneven lighting in your photo.

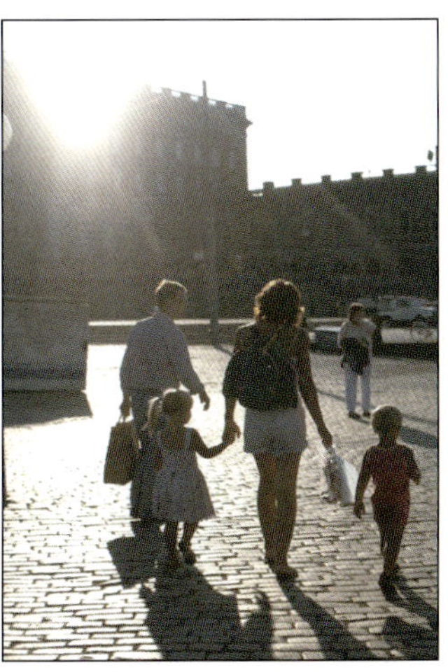

- Flare can be avoided in many cases by shading the lens of your camera from the sun. The easiest way to do this is ask a friend to help by blocking the sun with their hand or a magazine. You can do it yourself with a few contortions.
- When blocking the sun, be careful not to accidentally include your hand in the picture.
- Flare can also occur if you have a bright light source (such as the sun) in the picture.

Grainy Prints

Grain can best be described as seeing the dots that make up the picture. Possible causes of grainy pictures are:

- You are using a very high-speed film, especially an off-brand.
- You had your film push-processed to compensate for underexposure.
- Your picture is underexposed. Underexposed images often have a grainy, hazy feel.

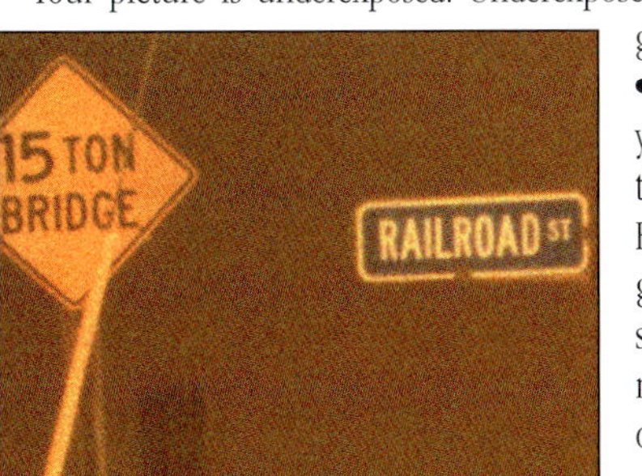

- You have enlarged your negative beyond the recommended size. Higher speed films are grainier, and cannot be successfully enlarged as much as pictures taken on slow-speed films.

• If your picture is digital, then graininess becomes "pixelation." You have enlarged this picture beyond the recommended size. You need to have a higher resolution digital picture to eliminate this problem.
• What problem? Many photographers use grain to their creative advantage. Sometimes it lends an artistic feel to the picture.

Light Prints

These are some common causes of light prints:
• If your subject is very dark, such as a black cat on a dark couch, it can be difficult for even a sophisticated camera to expose it correctly. Fortunately, most print films can produce acceptable images even if the exposure wasn't perfect. Ask your photofinisher to try making a darker print.
• Flash Range: You are closer to your subject than the recommended flash range (such as three feet away), and the power flash over-lights the subject.
• The photofinishing lab printed the images too light.

Marks on Prints

• White dust specs or hairs on the print, means the negative was dirty when it was printed. Ask to have the negative cleaned and reprinted.
• Sometimes specular highlights on shiny objects look like dust.
• White lines indicate scratches on the print. The rollers on the processing machine may have dragged a piece of debris along the soft surface of the paper, thereby scratching it.
• Flash pictures in rain or snow often have white dots, caused when the flash bounces off the shiny water droplets or bright white snow flakes.

Dark marks are more problematic.
• A scratch on the negative will show up as a black spot on the print. If the negative is scratched, digital retouching is probably your best option to minimize it.
• Prints made from slides (instead of negatives) will have black spots instead of white spots if they are dirty.
• If you scanned a negative to make a digital file, the negative may have been dirty.

• A scanner with a dirty glass surface may add dark marks to your digitally scanned picture.

Miscut Prints

• Sometimes the prints on an automated machine get misaligned and your prints come back with a black edge (actually the frame dividing two pictures) or they are completely miscut. Have them reprinted.

• If this happens more than once, ask the lab to view your negatives. The spaces between picture frames should be even. If they're not, your camera could have problems with its film advance system.

Photo Credits

Linda M. Alexander: 88
Colleen Arcand:3
Clara Luz Linan Azura: 34 (bottom)
Louise Bates: 68 (center)
Terrance Bechal: 14, 30
Wendy E. Bell: 45
Jenni Bidner: 7, 22, 32, 36, 60 (top), 61 (bottom), 63 (top), 66, 67, 68 (top), 69 (top), 73, 78,
Warner Blackburn: 60 (bottom)
Don Blair for PhotoAlley.com: 9 (bottom)
Debbie L. Booth: 54
Cindy E. Brennan: 52 (bottom right)
Wilson Bressler: 76
Bill Cafer: 71 (bottom)
Cesar M. Celadon: 52 (top)
Jim Companik: 68 (bottom)
Cheryl Croston: 19, 26, 40, 44 (top), 55(bottom), 61 (top, center), 62 (top)
Susan E. Drey: 46
Alan Farkas: 43 (top)
Ed Fortuna:41
Rodolfo de la Fuente: 35
Annette Feuz: 65 (bottom)
Glenn Gaffney: 39 (bottom)
Edwin G. Giacomozzi: 57 (top)
Larry C. Graff: 28 (bottom)
Kamie Graves: 56 (top)
Josee Griffin: 47
Robin L. Griffin: 9 (top)
Jane Huzar:83 (top)
Nicolas Y. Jimenez: 74
Dwayne Jones: 62 (bottom)
Steve Kelly: 37, 42, 43 (bottom), 50, 58
Tara Lee Kohlman: 20 (top)
Steve Krepps: 16
Janice Laulainen: 65 (top)
Gordon Llewellyn: 33
Paulina Robles Madrigal: 64
Gary Maritke: 48
De Alvarez McIntosh: 34 (center)
Robert Mccann: 39 (top)
Carol Murphy: 83 (bottom)
John Myers: 56 (bottom), 87, 100
Karen M. Ours: 8
Marion Quennell: 51
Annette Panebianco: 69 (bottom)
Rebecca Anne Parker: 4
Yvonne Parmentier: 53 (center), 55 (top)
Isabelle Pellerin: front cover
Dean Pennala: 34 (top)
Rod Perchak: 28 (top)
Wilma Pollock: 52 (bottom left)
Nathalie Poirer: 70 (top)
Stacey L. Poythress: 49
Paula Ruth Priest: 80
Jennifer Saltzman: 53 (bottom)
Laura H. Sandall: 62 (center)
Janet Sarver: 10
Susan B. Scopie: 53 (top)
Susan Simmons: 63 (bottom)
Theresa Spillett: 38
Susan Riley Stewart: 81
Bernardo Z. Taylor: 21 (top)
Selby Greer Thomas: 20 (bottom)
Lynn M. Trella: 44 (bottom)
Arnold Vandenburgh: 75
Pedro R. Vega: 77
Tina Wheatley: 21 (bottom)
Gary Whelpley: 11
Peg Williams: 71 (top)
Glenda Sherman Wyatt: 23
Christine M. Yesko: 70 (bottom)
Javier Zaletas: 72 (bottom)